W9-BUD-282

WARREN BUFFETT

SPEAKS

Wit and Wisdom

from

the

World's

Greatest Investor

~ * ~

WARREN BUFFETT SPEAKS

Wit and Wisdom

from

the

World's

Greatest Investor

JANET LOWE

John Wiley & Sons, Inc.

New York • Chichester • Weinheim • Brisbane • Singapore • Toronto

Copyright © 1997 by Janet C. Lowe
Published by John Wiley & Sons, Inc.

Library of Congress Cataloging-in-Publication Data:

Lowe, Janet C.
    Warren Buffett speaks : wit and wisdom from the world's greatest
investor / Janet C. Lowe.
        p.   cm.
    ISBN 0-471-16996-X (alk. paper)
    1. Buffett, Warren—Quotations. 2. Capitalists and financiers—
United States—Biography. I. Lowe, Janet. II. Title.
HG172.B84B84 1997
332.6—dc20   96-38904

Book design by Anne Scatto/PIXEL PRESS

Printed in the United States of America

10 9 8 7 6 5 4 3 2 1

~ ✳ ~

To my patient family.

JCL

~ ✳ ~

CONTENTS

ACKNOWLEDGMENTS

Many generous people helped in the preparation of this book. Thanks to Susan T. Buffett; Pam Buffett; Warren Buffett; Jolene Crowley; Elizabeth Douglass; *San Diego Union-Tribune;* Lorena Goeller; Arthur Q. Johnson; Steve Jorden; *Omaha World-Herald;* Irving Kahn, Kahn Brothers; Kathy Lowe; Austin Lynas; Bruce Marks; The North Carolina Public Television Foundation and the Kenan-Flagler School of Business, University of North Carolina, Chapel Hill; William J. Ruane, founder of the Sequoia Fund; Walter Schloss of Walter & Edwin Schloss; R. Hutchings Vernon; Kathy Welton; my editor Myles Thompson; and my literary agent Alice Fried Martell.

INTRODUCTION

JANET LOWE

Is there anyone anywhere who has more nicknames than Warren Buffett? *Vanity Fair* calls him the Forrest Gump of finance.[1] He's been dubbed the Oracle of Omaha, Omaha's plain dealer, the corn-fed capitalist, St. Warren (with a less than admiring inflection) and the financial world's Will Rogers.

Several books attempt to capture the personality, philosophy, and the very essence of the world's most successful investor, but words fail to adequately describe this unique individual. Except perhaps his own words. Nobody does Warren Buffett as well as Warren Buffett. It was this realization that inspired this collection of his aphorisms and observations.

There are many reasons to pick up a book on Buffett, but one of the best is to try to learn from him. Buffett warns that there is no quick and easy way to get rich; nevertheless, he did indeed get very rich; and although it may not have been via a quick or easy path, most of us would like to understand how he got there. If you pay close attention to what Buffett says, while you probably will not become exactly like him, you might grow wiser. You also could become a smarter, saner investor.

Who is this modern American hero/questionable saint? Here are the basics. The details will unfold as you read the rest of the book . . . told in his own words.

Warren Edward Buffett was born August 30, 1930 in Omaha, Nebraska. He attended grade school there, but went to junior high and high school in the Washington, D.C. area where his father Howard Homan Buffett served four terms in the U.S. House of Representatives. In college, Warren Buffett abandoned the Wharton School at the University of Pennsylvania because he didn't think he was learning anything. He enrolled in the University of Nebraska (Lincoln campus) where he earned a bachelor of science degree in 1950. He then applied to Harvard but was rejected. Instead, Buffett earned a master of science in economics from Columbia in 1951. It was at Columbia that he met the great investor, Professor Benjamin Graham, who soon became Buffett's mentor and friend.

He married Susan Thompson, an Omaha neighbor, in 1952. The couple raised three children, one daughter and two sons. The Buffetts have resided in separate cities for many years. They seem to be a close and affectionate couple, but their relationship puzzles many people.

Susan Buffett, who with her husband owns a majority interest in Berkshire Hathaway, is a vivacious, empathetic person, whom Buffett has described as "a free spirit." She lives in San Francisco where she strives to maintain as normal and balanced a life as possible, despite the wealth and fame that has descended upon her. "I have a quiet life of my own with my family and people I love." Buffett lives in Omaha where he has a woman companion and devotes his time to Berkshire Hathaway. The Buffetts say they are as close as ever and often travel together.

Buffett's salary as chairman of Berkshire is $100,000 per year with perks, which in 1993 amounted to $248,000. This made Buffett the lowest-paid executive among the largest 200 companies in the country, though that year he also was the nation's wealthiest man by virtue of his majority interest in Berkshire. In addition to his apparently substantial, though undisclosed personal investments, Buffett owns 25 percent of the Omaha Royals, a minor league baseball team.

Buffett's professional record speaks for itself. His first investment fund, the Buffett Partnership, ran from 1956 to 1969 with a record of 32 percent average annual return before fees. Shortly after the 100-member partnership closed, Buffett began transforming Berkshire Hathaway from a textile manufacturer into a holding company/investment vehicle that has no exact parallel on Wall Street. When Buffett bought his first 2,000 shares of Berkshire Hathaway the stock was selling at $7.50 per share, plus 10 cents per share commission. Buffett had taken control of the company in 1965, when shares were trading at $12 and $15. In its 31 years under Buffett's tutelage, Berkshire's market price rose to over $38,000 per share (at the time of this writing it had retreated to around $32,000). Berkshire's per-share book value has grown at a rate of more than 23 percent compounded annually, which is nearly three times the gains in major stock averages.

Dozens of people who invested with Buffett when he first started managing money remain with him today—or their heirs do. If an investor had given Buffett $10,000 to manage in 1956 and had reinvested all profits, by the end of 1994, that person would hold stock worth $80 million.

Despite his influence and affluence, Buffett is an "aw shucks" kind of guy. He is plainspoken, honest, optimistic, and funny. He follows a simple wisdom, but it would be a mistake to underestimate his intelligence, knowledge, or resolve. Buffett sets very tough standards and sticks to them.

The Economist described Buffett's style in handling the Salomon Inc. U.S. government bond scandal as "fast, frank, and folksy,"[2] and that's pretty much how he talks. He may sound homey and slow, but try taking notes. You'll be reduced to the crudest of shorthand. Trust me, I've tried.

Though Buffett is invariably polite, he does not spend time on projects, concepts, or people unless they interest him, seem worthy, or relate to his bottom line. He can be impatient when his patience is tried. For example, though he seldom couches his criticism in personal terms, Buffett has few kind words for academicians who chase one investment theory after another, failing to acknowledge the basic, underlying economic function of stocks and the stock market. He cuts no slack for advisers who lure investors into speculative ventures.

Buffett is a friendly, talkative guy, and when he speaks or writes, people enjoy listening. In 1996, nearly 6,000 shareholders, family members, and friends crowded into Omaha to attend Berkshire's annual meeting and to hear him. Every year, they gather at the Red Lion, the Radisson, and a handful of other hotels to compare returns. The ones with the earliest Berkshire Hathaway purchase dates are the winners. Needless to say, many of these people are repeat visitors to Omaha.

R. Hutchings Vernon, an analyst with Alex. Brown Investment Management in Baltimore explained what has happened: "Ten years ago, when I first attended the annual meeting and the shares were trading around $2,500, there were perhaps 400 shareholders in attendance (a large number in comparison to most annual meetings). Five years before that, with the stock around $500 per share, there were reportedly only 15 in attendance. The 6,000 or so shareholders at the 1996 event is unparalleled."

Vernon later concluded that Buffett's " ... comments and writings over the years are, in my view, the most important lessons for anyone involved with business, finance, or investing."[3]

William Ruane, founder of the Sequoia Fund, has been a friend of Buffett's since they met in Benjamin Graham's seminar at Columbia University. Ruane describes Buffett's speaking skills this way. "Warren is a genius, but he can explain something so simply and with such clarity that, at least at that moment, you understand exactly what he's saying."

"Warren's gift is being able to think ahead of the crowd," writes his buddy Bill Gates, chief executive of Microsoft, "and it requires more than taking his aphorisms to heart to accomplish that—although Warren is full of aphorisms worth taking to heart."[4]

Once, however, Buffett's storytelling habit brought a rap on the knuckles. He was testifying as an expert witness in a federal case, and the attorney asked him a question. "Please Mr. Buffett," the judge interjected. "Not another story." Buffett protested that this was his manner of communicating. The judge sighed and Buffett spun his yarn.[5]

By way of disclosure, I have interviewed and met Buffett a number of times and admit to liking him. This may lead the reader to assume that I will try to present Buffett in the best light. That is not my objective. It is my goal to demonstrate his unusual way of thinking and let the reader make value judgments for her or himself. I've included incidents where Buffett's behavior is difficult to understand, along with points of view of those who don't think he's so terrific. Nevertheless, I admit the material is presented in a mostly friendly light. After all, if I didn't think Buffett had wonderfully useful things to say, I would not have spent so much time and energy on this book. He is interesting; he is funny; and he makes people think about the world in unexpected ways. Considering the enormous pressure now put upon him by a wide range of "others," he does a commendable job of being himself.

A cheerful good humor and lack of malice dominate Buffett's personality. His parents obviously told him that if he couldn't say something nice about a person, not to say anything at all, and he believed it. But there is also a subtle quality to his demeanor that implies he means what he does say. Although he is open to ideas, unless you have something new, constructive, and convincing to add to his information, he is unlikely to be swayed. Some people gain this kind of self-confidence with age; Buffett apparently has long been sure of what he thought and is ready to defend his ideas.

It may be helpful to have instructions on how to read this book. This compilation of Buffett's quotations could be called a *Life's Little Lesson Book* for investors. The sayings (plus anecdotes by and about Buffett) are organized under broad general categories, and beneath those categories are specific headings. The topic headings are followed by one or more quotations, a little story, or a short account of an event. When necessary, I have set the quotation in its proper perspective. Each quote is a small clue to the philosophy by which Buffett lives while creating and managing his wealth (not to mention creating wealth for others). Included are segments about significant friends, family, colleagues, and events: what these people and incidents say about Buffett; what the players have to say about themselves and their role in the Buffett saga.

Even though the collection is conversational in tone, please remember that this is a collage. The comments did not necessarily occur in the order listed here, nor were comments on related topics necessarily made at the same time.

I have tried to give the reader a sense of Buffett's personality through selection, placement, and treatment of the quotes. His comments don't always translate perfectly from the speaking to the reading, sorry to say. To a certain extent, it's Buffett's delivery that makes his comments so entertaining. Though Buffett speaks well, when he is relaxed and talking without notes—which is always—his grammar is not perfect. But whose is? He "uhs" and "ums" his way through a statement and then repeats himself. He can speak for ten minutes without ending a sentence, each phrase connected by "and." In many cases, I've quoted him verbatim, leaving it up to the reader to sort out the misplaced modifiers, and so on. In these cases, the exact wording seems the best way to get the point across. When possible, I've emphasized the words that he emphasized.

In an occasional rare instance, for the sake of clarity and space, I copy-edited ever so slightly. "Ums" and "ahs" were eliminated, or the noun and verb were made to match in terms of past and present, plural or singular. In almost all cases, the change is in parentheses. This was done with meticulous care to preserve Buffett's intention and meaning. It is important to Buffett that he be understood clearly. I was once with him at a press conference in New York. Several hours after he spoke, Buffett was given a copy of a wire service story that had been distributed reporting his comments. There was a small but rather significant error in the story. "I don't think I said that. Did I say that? No, I don't think I did." He was clearly disturbed by the idea that this misquotation would be repeated worldwide, would most likely go into many, many research databases and in time be chiseled in marble.

Knowing that errors have been made and knowing how Warren Buffett feels about that, the book was submitted to him to correct or clarify any mistakes, whether borrowed or my own. Quotations that conveyed an incorrect meaning were changed. Whenever it appeared that a quotation was or could be misinterpreted, the discrepancy is discussed in the text.

In compiling this book, I have noticed some intriguing patterns. For example, Buffett started measuring many things—the price of his wife's engagement ring for example—in terms of net worth at an age when most people don't know how to figure their net worth, and if they did know how, would come up with a negative number. He also likes the "pretend you're going away for (five, ten, etc.) years" construct.

He writes his annual reports to a sister who has been on an extended vacation, or suggests investing as if you wouldn't be able to change your mind for a decade. Punching tickets and accumulating claim checks are commonly used Buffett metaphors.

Readers may observe patterns that I have missed. It will be interesting to see how others interpret and what they glean from *Warren Buffett Speaks*. My overriding observation is that despite the fondness of some reporters to view Buffett as a midwestern bumpkin, this man is no bumpkin. After reading correspondence between Buffett and his mentor Benjamin Graham, I suspect that Buffett purposely retains his homespun language and explains things in parable form to better communicate with us mere mortals. When he lets loose with his full vocabulary and intellect, many of us would be left eating dust.

Willa Cather fans will recognize immediately in Buffett the unpretentious intelligence, balance, depth, and sense of authority over oneself that the Nebraska-reared novelist saw in her fellow plainspeople. Cather did not claim, however, that heartlanders were simple in their psychology or unflawed in their nature. This said, it is up to each of us to decide for ourselves who the real Warren Buffett is.

~

When I told Buffett that I would be doing this book, he responded in his typical, cordial way: "I know you will do a good job." In a later letter, he outlined his usual position when books are written about him. He would send a letter to friends and family telling them to cooperate or not cooperate, whichever they prefer.

He noted, however, that he was saving his copyrighted material for his own book, which all Buffett fans pant for. It is my hope, though not my claim, that this book will complement his. It is also my hope that you enjoy reading *Warren Buffett Speaks* as much as I've enjoyed working on it.

ABOUT LIFE

When Warren Buffett speaks on stock markets, business ethics, or the price of corn in Nebraska, ears perk up all over the world. His words often have relevance beyond the immediate issue. They bring forth an "Ah ha!" or "Of course!" Buffett's comments seem to touch many aspects of our lives. Though he ranks among the wealthiest people in the world, his friend Charlie Munger says that Buffett also is one of the happiest people he knows. Before reading what Buffett has to say about successful investing, let's see what he says about the more important subjects of living productively and being content.

LIVE WHERE YOU'RE HAPPIEST

Warren Buffett—or "Fireball" as his dad called him—spent his early years attending public school in Omaha. When his father, Howard Buffett, was elected to the House of Representatives, the family moved to the nation's capital. Young Warren pined to go back home:

"I was miserably homesick. I told my parents I couldn't breathe when lying down. I told them not to worry about it, to get a good night's sleep themselves, and I'd just stand up all night."

Eventually, 12-year-old Warren was allowed to return to Omaha to live with his grandfather until the end of the school term.[6]

~

Buffett later attended Wharton School of Business at the University of Pennsylvania, graduate school at Columbia University, and worked for the Graham-Newman Company in New York, but in early 1956, at age 25, he went home to Omaha to stay:

"I've lived in New York and Washington, but the logistics of New York take a lot of time. I can get the pluses of New York and Los Angeles by getting on a plane and flying for three hours, but I pay no penalty by having to live there."[7]

~

"I think it's a saner existence here. I used to feel, when I worked back in New York, that there were more stimuli just hitting me all the time, and you've got the normal amount of adrenaline, you start responding to them. It may lead to crazy behavior after a while. It's much easier to think here."[8]

~

Buffett's younger son Peter, a musician, composed a song called "Nebraska." It expresses a similar love of America's heartland: "It expresses how strongly I feel about having the foundation, the solidity, the spiritual roots of a homeland," Peter Buffett said of his composition.

LIVE HOW YOU WANT TO LIVE

"One of the things that attracted me to working with securities was the fact that you could live your own life. You don't have to dress for success," said Warren Buffett. [9]

〜

"I can't think of anything in life I want that I don't have."[10]

〜

Is Buffett's lifestyle merely the path of least resistance for him?

"It's easier to create money than to spend it."[11]

EAT WHAT YOU WANT TO EAT

If we are what we eat, Buffett is all-American:

"My ideas about food and diet were irrevocably formed quite early—the product of a wildly successful party that celebrated my fifth birthday. On that occasion we had hot dogs, hamburgers, soft drinks, popcorn, and ice cream."

Buffett's signature dish is a Dusty Sunday. He pours lots of Hershey's Chocolate Syrup over vanilla ice cream, then heaps malted milk power over that. He justifies the calories mathematically:

> *"The caloric consumption produced by this concoction is inconsequential. Assume that your basal metabolism rate is 2,800 calories per day. Simple arithmetic tells us that you can—indeed you must—consume slightly over 1 million calories per year. In my own case—with a life expectancy of about 25 years—this means that, in order to avoid premature death through starvation, I need to eat some 25 million calories. Why not get on with it?"[12]*

～

Mathematics also explain Buffett's Coca-Cola addiction:

> *"I drink five (Cherry Cokes) a day. That's 750 calories. I would have lost 70 pounds a year if I didn't drink them. Really, it's been a lifesaver."[13]*

～

There are times, however, when calories aren't worth the cost. Buffett once was offered a glass of high-priced wine at a dinner party. Holding his hand over his glass he replied:

> *"No thanks. I'll take cash."[14]*

～

HAVE A HOBBY

Investing is both sport and entertainment for Buffett. He likens finding a good acquisition to "bagging rare and fast-moving elephants."[15] He attends Omaha Royals baseball games; he gathers with family and friends for special occasions, such as to celebrate an award given by the Omaha YWCA to his daughter for her work on The Rose Theater, and for Bill Gates' wedding on the Hawaiian island of Lanai.

Every other year, he organizes a meeting of the Buffett Group, a gathering of his longest and dearest friends. Although he quit racquetball after injuring his back, he still occasionally plays golf, and at the 1996 annual meeting, a noticeably slimmer Buffett explained that he'd taken up working out on a treadmill.

Bridge has been Buffett's great passion, and recently, under the guidance of an expert coach, his card game has risen to new levels. He likes the game so much that he says:

"Any young person who doesn't take up bridge is making a big mistake."[16]

"I don't think about anything else when I play bridge."[17]

"I always said I wouldn't mind going to jail if I had three cellmates who played bridge."[18]

Buffett's bridge coach (Sharon Osberg, a world champion player whom he met through bridge-playing friend Carol Loomis) introduced him to the computer and to ImagiNation, a network that allows him to play cards from home with friends around the country.

> *"I'd walk by a PC and be afraid it might bite me, but once I got started it was easy. Bridge is the only thing I know how to do with the machine."*

~

Thanks to the computer, Buffett now cuts the deck with his sister and her husband who live in Carmel, California; distinguished friends in Washington, D.C.; and even William H. Gates Sr., the Seattle attorney whose famous son founded Microsoft Inc.:

> *"Now it is much easier to get the game up and running with the same people I usually played with, only now we all sit thousands of miles apart. I played for six hours one Sunday. I don't play as many face-to-face games anymore."[19]*

NOTE: I know Buffett's bridge-playing code name, but I won't tell. One hint: Buffett's on-line portrait, which ImagiNation allows the player to create him- or herself, looks peculiarly like Peter Lynch.

BE PASSIONATE

Passion sometimes involves spending money, as it did when Buffett bought his corporate jet, The Indefensible.

Buffett considered naming the plane The Charles T. Munger in honor of his partner, who still resolutely flies coach class:

> *"I've fallen in love with the plane. It's going to be buried with me."*[20]

After Buffett went to New York for nearly a year to work through problems at Salomon Inc., he began calling his plane "The Semidefensible."[21]

~

Buffett has had a lifetime love for cola drinks, first Pepsi-Cola and later Coca-Cola (Cherry Coke to be precise). The Buffett's once threw a party, and Susie Buffett decorated the entrance with 3-foot tall Pepsi bottles in the front windows.

"Everybody who knows Warren knows he doesn't have a bloodstream—it's a Pepsi stream; he even has it for breakfast," his wife said.

AIM HIGH

Now that you are the richest man in America, asked a shareholder at a Berkshire Hathaway annual meeting, what is your next goal? "That's easy," Buffett replied. "To be the oldest man in America."[22]

~

But don't overreach:

> *"I don't try to jump over 7-foot bars: I look around for 1-foot bars that I can step over."*[23]

~ ✳ ~

ATTENTION INVESTORS:
WARREN BUFFETT IS CROSSING THE STREET

At the 1996 annual meeting, an investor asked what would happen to Berkshire Hathaway if Buffett were to get hit by a truck. The question pops up more often than toast at breakfast. "I usually say I feel sorry for the truck," Buffett sometimes quips. Over the years he's tried various comebacks: [24]

1984: "If something happened to me tomorrow, Berkshire Hathaway will not be sold and parts of it will not be sold."[25]

1985: In an article about Berkshire's long-term commitment to the companies it acquires, Buffett noted: "...the managers have a corporate commitment and therefore need not worry if my personal participation in Berkshire's affairs ends prematurely (a term I define as any age short of three digits)."[26]

1986: "This is the proverbial 'truck' question that I get asked every year. If I get run over by a truck today, Charlie (Munger) would run the business, and no Berkshire stock would need to be sold. Investments would continue. There would be no surprises in the company's management. The company would last a long time in the present form."

Also, Buffett surmised that the stock might "move up a quarter or a half point on the day that I go. I'll be disappointed if it goes up a lot."[27]

1991: "Our businesses run as if I'm not there, so the exact location of my body shouldn't matter."[28]

1993: Even the media reminds Buffett of his mortality. A television reporter asked how he'd like to be remembered: "Well, I'd like for the minister to say, 'My God, he was old.'"[29]

1994: "I have publicly announced I plan to run Berkshire until 5 or 10 years after I die. But Berkshire is pretty easy to run."[30]

1995: "I'm thinking of making a purchase of Berkshire," said a member of the audience at the annual meeting, "but I'm concerned about something happening to you. I cannot afford an event risk."

"Neither can I," Buffett replied.

1996: When queried about the future of the company in case of his departure, Buffett said that should anything happen to him, Louis Simpson, the high-achieving investment director and co-president of GEICO would take over the investment function at Berkshire Hathaway.

Buffett has said his demise may even be good for some segments of the business:

"There actually will be a short-term bulge (in Coca-Cola sales) as I plan to have a large supply buried with me aboard the plane."[31]

Coca-Cola's share price might rise, but so would airplane sales:

"Upon my death Berkshire's earnings will immediately increase by $1 million, since Charlie will sell the corporate jet the next day, ignoring my wish to be buried with The Indefensible."[32]

AIM WELL

Invest the same way an expert plays hockey, says Buffett:

"Like Wayne Gretzky says, go where the puck is going, not where it is."[33]

~

"To swim a fast 100 meters, it's better to swim with the tide than to work on your stroke."[34]

FOCUS ON YOUR GOALS

"If we get on the main line, New York to Chicago, we don't get off at Altoona and take side trips."[35]

~

"I've often felt there might be more to be gained by studying business failures than business successes. It's customary in business schools to study business successes. But my partner, Charles Munger, says all he wants to know is where he's going to die—so he won't ever go there."[36]

KEEP LIFE IN PERSPECTIVE

Buffett had a notepad on his desk that read:

"In the event of nuclear war, disregard this message."[37]

~

In 1985, commenting on investments resulting in a 22 percent compounded growth for 20 years:

"It has been like overcoming a misspent youth."[38]

~

At a cocktail party, a tipsy woman approached Buffett and cooed, "I see money hanging all over you."

Buffett told a reporter:

"I don't measure my life by the money I've made. Other people might, but I certainly don't."[39]

~

"Money, to some extent, sometimes lets you be in more interesting environments. But it can't change how many people love you or how healthy you are."[40]

~ ✳ ~

NICE GUYS FINISH FIRST— SOMETIMES

"We've seen oil magnates, real estate moguls, shippers, and robber barons at the top of the money heap, but Buffett is the first person to get there just by picking stocks," says *Time* reporter John Rothchild.[41] Rothchild failed to mention that Buffett didn't start with inherited money; he made it on his own. Buffett's progression to the top of the wealthiest Americans list no doubt will become an American legend. Forget Horatio Alger stories. From now on, successful self-made people will be called "Warren Buffett" stories. Step by step, this is how he climbed up the Forbes 400 list of wealthiest Americans, starting in 1982:

1982: Warren Buffett ranked number 82 with $250 million. Daniel K. Ludwig was first on the list with $2 billion, and Gordon Peter Getty was number 2 with $1.4 billion.

1983: Buffett jumped to 31 by doubling his net worth to $520 million. Getty rose to number 1 with $2.2 billion, and Sam Walton ranked second with $2.15 billion.

1984: Buffett was number 23 with holdings worth $665 million. First again was Getty with $4.1 billion. Second was Sam Walton, now worth $2.3 billion.

1985: BUFFETT BECOMES NEBRASKA'S FIRST BILLIONAIRE WITH $1.07 BILLION.[42] He ranked 12 on the Forbes 400. Walton made the top with $2.8 billion. Ross Perot was number 2 with $1.8 billion.

1986: Gaining on the competition was Buffett, in fifth place with a net worth of $1.4 billion. Sam Walton held the lead with $4.5 billion, and John Kluge took second with $2.5 billion.

In 1986, *U.S. News & World Report* also published a list of 100 individuals and families who owned the biggest stakes in America's publicly traded companies. Buffett ranked eighth, with the Walton family at the top. Buffett observed:

"Did you see how precise they tried to be? The only thing is, they forgot to allow for a couple of burgers that I bought at Bronco's last night."[43]

1987: Worth $2.1 billion, Buffett dropped to number 7. Walton and Kluge again were the first and second richest men in America.

1988: Buffett's net worth rose to $2.2 billion, but he dropped to ninth place. Again, Walton, with $6.7 billion, and Kluge, with $3.2 billion, were in the lead.

1989: Buffett sped ahead to second place with $4.2 billion. John Kluge was number 1 with $5.2 billion. The leader worldwide was Yoshiaki Tsutsumi, a Japanese developer worth $15 billion.

1990: Again Buffett was in second place, worth $3.3 billion. Kluge was first with $5.6 billion.

1991: Lower on the list, but as rich as ever, Buffett took fourth place with $4.2 billion. Kluge again was in first place with $5.9 billion. A newcomer, Bill Gates, took second with $4.8 billion of net worth.

1992: Buffett was fourth again, with $4.3 billion. Gates leapt to first with $6.3 billion, and Kluge was second with $5.5 billion.

1993: NUMBER 1 WITH $8.3 BILLION. Bill Gates fell to second wealthiest American with $6.16 billion.[44]

1994: Back to second place, Buffett's wealth rose to only $9.2 billion. Gates led with $9.35 billion.

1995: Buffett was second again with $12 billion. Gates was the winner with $15 billion in net worth.

On the tug-of-war between Buffett and Gates for first or second richest person in the United States, satirist Art Buchwald observed: "Despite being friendly in each other's presence, there must be some tension between the two men. When you're number 1, you're always looking over your shoulder to see who is coming up from behind. On the other hand, when you're number 2, you spend all your time explaining to your family how you failed."[45]

BE HONEST

Buffett told his son Howard:

"It takes 20 years to build a reputation and five minutes to ruin it. If you think about that, you'll do things differently."[46]

~

"Never lie under any circumstances. Don't pay any attention to the lawyers. If you start letting lawyers get into the picture, they'll basically tell you, 'don't say anything.' You'll never get tangled up if you just basically lay it out as you see it."

~

Though he has a lifetime involvement with newspapers, Buffett says dealing with reporters can be risky:

"The tough part about it is that essentially there is no one, virtually with the exception of an assassin, that can do you as much damage as somebody can in the press, if they do something the wrong way. There may be doctors out there who can do you just as much harm, but in that case, you initiate the transaction."[47]

~

One misunderstanding with the media involved the *Lifestyles of the Rich and Famous* television show. Buffett's friends were more than a little surprised when he was featured on Robin Leach's program, since it's not Buffett's habit to parade his wealth.

"I was just as surprised as you were," Buffett

reportedly told friends. "I never heard from Robin Leach; we didn't even have a request to appear. Suddenly, we were just on the show."

Leach disputes that version of the story. "Buffett absolutely knew we were doing it. It wasn't a sit-down interview, but he approved. That's why we bill-boarded the show as an exclusive. It was."

NOTE: Actually Borsheim's jewelry store in Omaha invited *Lifestyles* to film a Patek Phillipe exhibition the Sunday before Berkshire Hathaway's annual meeting. Buffett agreed to talk to Robin Leach in conjunction with the exhibit. A film crew never came to his home and Buffett was unaware that a show was planned about him.[48]

An untruth can be accidental. There *was* the Nicholas Kenner affair. Buffett opened the 1990 annual meeting question-and-answer period by taking an inquiry from the 9-year-old New Yorker who then owned 11 shares of Berkshire. The youngster asked why Berkshire's stock price, at that time trading at about $6,600 per share, was so low. Buffett mentioned the question in his next annual letter to shareholders. Nicholas Kenner appeared at the next annual meeting with an even tougher question. Noting that since the annual report mistakenly reported that he was 11, when actually he was 9 years old, Kenner asked, "How do I know the numbers in the back (the financials) are correct?" Buffett promised a written response to the question.[49]

~

Little white lies are forgiven if they boost the sales of See's Candy, a company owned by Berkhire Hathaway.

"When business sags, we spread the rumor that our candy acts as an aphrodisiac. Very effective. The rumor, that is; not the candy."[50]

CULTIVATE GOOD CHARACTER

"Chains of habit are too light to be felt until they are too heavy to be broken."[51]

~

Character can be developed. Imagine, Buffett says, that you are a student, and you may choose one other student in your class, and thereafter be entitled to 10 percent of that student's earnings for life. But there's a catch. You also have to choose a student to whom you will pay 10 percent of your earnings for life:

"The interesting thing is, when you think about what's going through your mind, you're not thinking about things that are impossible for you to achieve yourself. You're not thinking about who can jump 7 feet, who can throw a football 65 feet, who can recite pi to 300 digits, or whatever it might be. You're thinking about a whole lot of qualities of character. The truth is, that every one of those qualities is obtainable. They are largely a matter of habit. My old boss, Ben Graham, when he was 12 years old, wrote down all of the qualities that he admired in other people and all the qualities

he found objectionable. And he looked at that list and there wasn't anything about being able to run the 100-yard dash in 9.6 or jumping 7 feet. They were all things that were simply a matter of deciding whether you were going to be that kind of person or not."[52]

~

"Someone's sitting in the shade today because someone planted a tree a long time ago."[53]

BELIEVE IN YOURSELF

When 20-year-old Buffett went to work at his father's brokerage house in Omaha, a friend asked if the company would be called Buffett & Son. "No," replied Buffett, "Buffett & Father."[54]

~

In a matter-of-fact way, Buffett says:

"I've never had any self-doubt. I've never been discouraged."[55]

~

"I always knew I was going to be rich. I don't think I ever doubted it for a minute."[56]

~

When 26-year-old Warren Buffett created his first partnership in 1956, he told investors: "What I'll do is form a partnership where I'll manage the portfolio and have my money in there with you. I'll guarantee you a 5 percent return, and I'll get 20 percent of all profits after that. And I won't tell you what we own because that's distracting. All I want to do is hand in a scorecard when I come off the golf course. I don't want you following me around and watching me shank a three-iron on this hole and leave a putt short on the next one."[57]

NOTE: Apparently, the preceding is someone's recollection of what Buffett said. Buffett did not guarantee a 5 percent return. The partnership gave the limited partners a preferential return that had to be achieved on a cumulative basis before Buffett earned anything.

∼

"I keep an internal *scoreboard. If I do something that others don't like but I feel good about, I'm happy. If others praise something I've done, but I'm not satisfied, I feel unhappy."*[58]

∼

When asked how he has the confidence to invest in companies that others shun:

"In the end, I always believe my eyes rather than anything else."[59]

BUT DON'T GET TOO STUCK ON YOURSELF

Probably the majority of people felt like Buffett did in high school:

"I would not have been the most popular guy in the class, but I wouldn't have been the most unpopular either. I was just sort of nothing."[60]

~

When Buffett graduated from Columbia, he asked Benjamin Graham for a job (for no salary) at the Graham-Newman Co.:

"Ben made his customary calculation of value to price and said no."[61]

~

Buffett pitches the opening ball at Omaha Royals games preceding the Berkshire Hathaway annual meetings. Before one game, Buffett said, children asked for his autograph. After his pitch, which was a little weak:

"I looked up and saw these same kids erasing my signature."[62]

~

Wounded by a journalist who said Buffett wore cheap suits, he explained:

"I buy expensive suits. They just look cheap on me."[63]

NOTE: After years of wearing mostly cotton shirts, slacks, and a blazer, Buffett started dressing up. He wears Italian-made Zegna suits, usually off the rack. Zegnas sell for about $1,500. [64]

~

Upon induction to the Omaha Business Hall of Fame, Buffett said he wanted to thank his hair stylist, his wardrobe consultant, and his personal trainer, but:

"When they looked at their handiwork, they asked to remain anonymous."[65]

⟋

When the Omaha Press Club unveiled a caricature by artist James Horan, Buffett laughed:

"Almost anything beats looking in the mirror."[66]

⟋

The governor of Nebraska and Buffett performed a skit together, in which the governor announced the winning numbers for a Nebraska state lottery, and Buffett dashed onto stage waving the winning stub. The governor asked Buffett what he would do with the windfall: "I think I'll buy a second suit," the excited Buffett stuttered, then added. "And if I have enough left over, I'll buy a comb."[67]

⟋

Buffett's business partner Charlie Munger says, "Buffett's tailoring has caused a certain amount of amusement in the business world."[68]

⟋

Buffett has found a corporate jet to be a true convenience, but he's not letting the plane go to his head: "Whatever colors were on the corporate jet when we bought it are the ones that are on it today. There's no WB or BH and that's not likely to change."[69]

~

When a shareholder asked Buffett if he was aware of how popular he had become, Buffett replied: "Maybe I should tell my barber and we should save the clippings."[70]

~

When it was suggested to Buffett that as a folk hero, some people watch his every move: "I watch my every move and I'm not that impressed."[71]

~ ✳ ~

CHOOSE YOUR HEROES WELL

"You're lucky in life if you have the right heroes. I advise all of you, to the extent that you can, pick out a few heroes. There's nothing like the right ones," Buffett says.

Among his champions Buffett lists his father Howard, mentor Ben Graham, and author Phil Fisher. Why these people? [72]

HOWARD HOMAN BUFFETT

"He taught me to do nothing that could be put on the front page of a newspaper. I have never known a better human being than my dad."[73]

NOTE: Buffett later said that what he meant was that his father told him never to do anything that would make him or his family unhappy if it was chronicled on the front page of a newspaper.

~

Buffett's mother explained the relationship between father and son: "Warren and his father were always the best of friends. His dad was Warren's hero. Howard was a wonderful husband and father. He never found it necessary to punish the children. His method was to use reason and persuasion."[74]

~

Buffett recalls a hometown baseball game shortly after his father had cast an unpopular House of Representatives vote on a labor measure. When Congressman Buffett was introduced, the crowd booed: "He could take stuff like that very well. He didn't expect the world to change overnight."[75]

~

Buffett's father was a staunch Republican and a member of the John Birch Society. Yet Buffett did not adopt his father's politics:

> *"I became a Democrat basically because I felt the Democrats were closer by a considerable margin to what I felt in the early '60s about civil rights. I don't vote the party line, but I probably vote more for Democrats than Republicans."*[76]

~

> *"I'm sort of a Republican on the production side, and I'm sort of a Democrat on the distribution side."*[77]

PHIL FISHER

One of the great original thinkers of modern investment management, Fisher is the author of *Common*

Stocks and Uncommon Profits and *Conservative Investors Sleep Well*. Buffett describes his own style as 85 percent Ben Graham and 15 percent Fisher:[78] "From him I learned the value of the 'scuttlebutt' approach: Go out and talk to competitors, suppliers, customers to find out how an industry or a company really operates."[79]

NOTE: Fisher's son Kenneth writes a column for *Forbes* magazine.

BILL GATES

"I'm not competent to judge his technical ability, but I regard his business savvy as extraordinary," Buffett says. "If Bill had started a hot dog stand, he would have become the hot dog king of the world. He will win in any game. He would be very good at my business, but I wouldn't be at his."[80]

~

As for the future of Gates and Microsoft in the shifting sands of computer software?

"I'd just bet on him. Nobody has lost money doing that yet."[81]

BENJAMIN GRAHAM

"Graham was the smartest man I ever knew," Buffett said.[82] For more on <u>Ben Graham, turn to page 88.</u>

July 12
2018

NOTE: Rose Blumkin, founder of the Nebraska furniture Mart, and all teachers rank high on Buffett's list. More about them later.

~ ✳ ~

DODGE THE HYPE

> *"Maybe grapes from a little 8-acre vineyard in France are really the best in the whole world, but I have always had a suspicion that about 99 percent of it is in the telling and about 1 percent is in the drinking."*[83]

SHARE YOUR WISDOM

When Bill Gates became engaged to be married, he flew his betrothed to Omaha to buy an engagement ring at Borsheim's, a jewelry store owned by Berkshire.

"Not to give you advice or anything," said Buffett, who is known for his unabashed promotion of his own companies, "but when I bought an engagement ring for my wife in 1951, I spent 6 percent of my net worth on it."[84] Though only 37 years old at the time, Gates already was a multibillionaire. Six percent of his net worth would have been around $500 million.

~

Buffett says he has no political aspirations, but that he can help elected officials set better goals. Rather than a balanced budget amendment, he proposes a "3 percent solution."

> *"Enact a constitutional amendment stipulating that every sitting representative and senator becomes ineligible for election if in any year of his term our budget deficit runs over 3 percent of the GDP (gross domestic product). Were this amendment passed, the interests of the nation and the personal interests of our legislators would instantly merge."*

This plan would serve the nation, Buffett says, because:

> *"It's not debt per se that overwhelms an individual, corporation, or country. Rather, it is a continuous increase in debt in relation to income that causes trouble."*

Other measures to control the national debt have failed because voters bounce elected officials who actually cut programs or increase taxes:

> *"There simply aren't enough saints available to staff a large institution that requires its members to voluntarily act against their own well-being."*[85]

DISREGARD OLD AGE

> *"Retirement plans? About 5 to 10 years after I die."*[86]

Buffett's attitude about his age also applies to those with whom he works:

> *"We take as our hero Methuselah."*[87]

Buffett compares the management at Coca-Cola to a winning team:

> *"If you have the 1927 Yankees, all you wish for is their immortality."*[88]

When Rose Blumkin hit 94, Buffett said he was forced to scrap his mandatory retirement-at-100 policy so that Mrs. B could continue to manage the Nebraska Furniture Mart, now owned by Berkshire, from the electric golf cart she steers everywhere. "My god. Good managers are so scarce I can't afford the luxury of letting them go just because they've added a year to their age."[89]

~

"We find it hard to teach a new dog old tricks. But we haven't had lots of problems with people who hit the ball out of the park year after year. Even though they're rich, they love what they do. And nothing ever happens to our managers. We offer them immortality."[90]

Immigrant from Russia

~ ✳ ~

ROSE BLUMKIN, MATRIARCH OF THE NEBRASKA FURNITURE MART

To Warren Buffett, 4-foot-10-inch, 102-year-old Rose Blumkin is an Omaha landmark. He recommends that visitors drop by and see her when they are in town. Mrs. B, as she is called in Omaha, is founder of the massive, modern, Nebraska Furniture Mart. Buffett often describes her common sense and work ethic when talking to graduate students and others studying business principles. Mrs. B, who never attended a day of school, immigrated from Russia alone at age 23 to join her husband in the United States.

Mrs. B's business motto has been "sell cheap and tell the truth."[91]

"If she ran a popcorn stand, I'd want to be in business with her," Buffett said. He bought the Nebraska Furniture Mart as a 53rd birthday present to himself.[92]

Mrs. B tells the story this way. "One day, he (Buffett) walks in and says to me, 'You want to sell me your store?' And I say, 'Yeah.' He says, 'How much do you want?' I say, '$60 million' He goes to the office and brings back a check. I say, 'You are crazy. Where are your lawyers? Where are your accountants?' He says, 'I trust you more.'"[93]

Later when an inventory was taken, the store was actually worth $85 million, but Mrs. B. did not raise the price. "I wouldn't go back on my word, but I was surprised. He never thought a minute. But he studies. I bet you he knew."[94]

Buffett had learned of Mrs. B's interest in selling the business and discussed the idea with her son, hoping not to offend Mrs. B when he approached her. The transaction was based on a one-page contract, no audits, and no inventories. The total legal and accounting fees were $1,400. The investment has been hugely successful.[95]

"I would rate him the best," Mrs. B said about Buffett.[96]

Sadly, however, a dispute erupted between Mrs. B and her family. The feud was hot news in Omaha, and the *Omaha World-Herald* reported every lurid detail. "She left the Nebraska Furniture Mart in a major-league snit May 3, 1989, contending that grandsons Ronald and Irvin Blumkin, company executives, were undercutting her authority in the carpet department."[97]

The entire family was aghast when Mrs. B called one of her grandsons a "Hitler."

Mrs. B was soon bored sitting at home, and in 1989 opened the 6-acre Furniture Warehouse across the street from the Nebraska Furniture Mart. She had no qualms doing this. "Warren Buffett is not my friend. I made him $15 million every year, and when I disagreed with my grandkids, he didn't stand up for me." As for the success of her new business, "I didn't open this store for money. I opened it for revenge."[98]

Mrs. B later made peace with her family, and forgave Buffett. She sold her new store and its 11-acre site to the Nebraska Furniture Mart for $4.94 million, putting her back in the fold. As part of the deal, Mrs. B continued to operate her carpet business within the store.

"I expect maybe too much," Mrs. B said of the family fracas. Running the warehouse was a strain and she sold because her son begged her not to work so hard.

"So I did. Five million dollars. And they paid cash. No credit. I love my kids," she said.

"I'd rather wrestle grizzlies than compete with Mrs. B and her progeny," Buffett said.[99]

Buffett admitted learning an important lesson from the episode. The second time, he asked Mrs. B for a lifetime noncompete clause, remedying a flaw in the Nebraska Furniture Mart purchase agreement of 10 years earlier. "I was young and inexperienced," the 62-year-old Buffett said.[100]

At the Omaha Press Club show in 1987 Buffett sang the following tribute to Rose Bumkin—to the tune of "Battle Hymn of the Republic":

Verse 1

Oh, we thought we'd make a bundle
When we purchased ABC
But we found it's not so easy
When your network's number three.
So now the load at Berkshire
Must be borne by Mrs. B.
Her cart is rolling on.

Chorus:

Glory, Glory, Hallelujah
Keep those buyers coming to ya.
If we get rich it must be through ya,
Her cart is rolling on.

Verse 2

Ideas flop and stocks may drop
But never do I pale
For no matter what my screwups
It's impossible to fail
Mrs. B will save me
She'll just throw another sale
Her cart is rolling on.

Verse 3

Forbes may think I'm brilliant
When they make their annual log.
But the secret is I'm not the wheel
But merely just a cog.
Without the kiss of Mrs. B.
I'd always be a frog.
Her cart is rolling on.[101]

ABOUT FRIENDS

KNOW WHAT FRIENDSHIP IS

"I have a half dozen close friends. Half male, half female, as it works out. I like them, admire them. There are no shells round them."[102]

~

How does Buffett define friendship?

"I remember asking that question of a woman who had survived Auschwitz. She said her test was, 'would they hide me?'"[103]

GO TO BAT FOR YOUR FRIENDS

"I ate lunch at the Omaha Club—that's the downtown club—and I noticed there weren't any Jews. I was told 'they have their own club.' Now, there are Jewish families that have been in Omaha a hundred years; they have contributed to the community all the time; they have helped build Omaha as much as anybody, and yet they can't join a club that John Jones, the new middle-

rank Union Pacific man, joins as soon as he's trans-
ferred here. That is hardly fair. *So I joined the Jewish*
club; it took me four months. They were a little put back
and confused, and I had to do some convincing. Then I
went back to the Omaha Club and told them that the
Jewish club wasn't totally Jewish any more. I got two
or three of the Jewish club members to apply to the
Omaha Club. Now we've got the thing cracked."[104]

BUILD LIFELONG FRIENDSHIPS

In 1968, Buffett and a group of his friends traveled to
Coronado, California, where they sought advice on
the stock market from their former Columbia professor, Ben Graham. To this day, the Buffett Group
continues to gather every other year: "They were
moderately well-to-do then. They are all rich now.
They haven't invented Federal Express or anything
like that. They just set one foot in front of the other.
Ben put it all down. It's just so simple."[105]

NOTE: Frugal Buffett originally suggested they find a
Holiday Inn, but the party stayed at the elegant
beachfront Hotel del Coronado.

CHARLIE MUNGER

Charles T. Munger, 73, is Buffett's combination best
friend/business partner. Like Buffett, Munger grew up
in Omaha, and as a teenager worked in Buffett's grandfather Ernest's grocery store.

"The Buffett family store provided a very desirable introduction of business," Munger said. "It required hard, accurate work over long hours, which caused many of the young workers, including me (and later Ernest's grandson Warren) to look for an easier career and to be cheerful upon finding disadvantages therein."[106]

Because Munger is about seven years older than Buffett, the two didn't meet until they were adults. Munger has been called the Buffett doppelgänger, though the description has its limits. Munger was admitted to Harvard Law School even though he didn't have an undergraduate degree; Buffett was rejected when he applied to Harvard Business School. A Republican, Munger gives money liberally to charitable causes, including the British antihunger group, Oxfam. Buffett, a Democrat, will leave virtually all of his money to a charitable trust, eventually to be used to help solve social problems.

Though Munger, unlike Buffett, isn't a particular fan of the Benjamin Graham investment philosophy, "I have been shaped tremendously by Charlie," Buffett says.[107]

Munger explains their synergy: "Everybody engaged in complicated work needs colleagues. Just the discipline of having to put your thoughts in order with somebody else is a very useful thing."[108]

A friend of the partners say that while Buffett is good at saying no, Munger is better. Buffett calls his friend "the abominable no man." To be sure, Munger has mastered short answers. "Charlie is not paid by the word," explains Buffett.[109]

Buffett further claims: "Charlie and I can handle a four-page memo over the phone with three grunts."[110]

Buffett describes his friend as his junior partner in good years and his senior partner in bad years, but that's just talk:[111] "Charlie is rational, very rational. He doesn't have his ego wrapped up in the business the way I do, but he understands it perfectly. Essentially, we have never had an argument, though occasional disagreements."[112]

Furthermore: "Charlie has the best 30-second mind in the world. He goes from A to Z in one move. He sees the essence of everything before you even finish the sentence."[113]

Buffett says it isn't necessary to be a rocket scientist to be a successful investor, though in Munger's estimation, Warren is plenty smart: "His brain is a superbly rational mechanism. And since he's articulate, you can see the damn brain working."[114]

Munger says Buffett is the same person in private that he is in public: "One of the reasons Warren is so cheerful is that he doesn't have to remember his lines."[115]

Munger says he can't recall Buffett ever getting angry: "Even when I took him fishing in Minnesota and upset the boat and we had to swim to shore, he didn't scream at me."[116]

When he gets around to it, Munger has good advice for investors: "There are huge advantages for an individual to get into a position where you make a few great investments and just sit back. You're paying less to brokers. You're listening to less nonsense."[117]

～

Munger wants more than rosy promises before Berkshire Hathaway invests in a company. Projections won't do: "They are put together by people who have an interest in a particular outcome, have a subconscious bias, and (their) apparent precision makes them fallacious. They remind me of Mark Twain's saying, 'A mine is a hole in the ground owned by a liar.' Projections in America are often lies, although not intentional ones, but the worst kind because the forecaster often believes them himself."[118]

Bull markets, Munger says, go to investor's heads: "If you're a duck on a pond, and it's rising due to a downpour, you start going up in the world. But you think it's you, not the pond."[119]

Munger isn't above a bit of silliness. When asked if he could play the piano: "I don't know. I've never tried."[120]

Munger say he and Buffett think so much alike that it's spooky.[121] Some of the differences between them, however, are striking: "In my whole life, nobody has ever accused me of being humble. Although humility is a trait I much admire, I don't think I quite got my full share."[122]

ABOUT FAMILY

DON'T SPOIL YOUR KIDS

"As Jesse Owens' (1936 Olympic gold medalist) child, your development would not be facilitated by letting you start 100-yard dashes at the 50-yard line."[123]

~

Munger explains Buffett's attitude on family in more detail: "Warren is just as tough on his children as he is on his employees. He doesn't believe that if you love somebody the way to do him good is to give him something he's not entitled to. And that's part of the Buffett personality."[124]

~

Buffett calls inherited wealth "food stamps for the rich."

"All these people who think that food stamps are debilitating and lead to a cycle of poverty, they're the same ones who go out and want to leave a ton of money to their kids."[125]

~

The rumor that Buffett has cut his children out of his will, however, is incorrect:

> *"They've gotten gifts right along, but they're not going to live the life of the super rich. I think they probably feel pretty good about how they've been brought up. They all function well, and they are all independent, in that they don't feel obliged to kowtow to me in any way."*[126]

~

After explaining his family philosophy to a group of college students, Buffett conceded:

> *"My kids will be glad to come and rebut this next week."*[127]

~

Buffett apparently believes his child-rearing practices brought good results:

> *"They've all gone their own ways to accomplish a lot. They're productive, and they don't expect to just be some rich guy's kid."*[128]

~

> *"I respect what my kids are doing, and I don't feel my lifestyle is superior to any of theirs. If they want to get involved in this business, fine, but I don't expect it. I do have a letter accompanying my will that says that, if any of my descendants show any*

interest in the business, they should be given a slight
priority, but only *a slight priority."¹²⁹*

~

A *slight* priority is right. When Buffett's son Howard
ran for county commissioner in Omaha, voters falsely
assumed that with his surname, his campaign would
be well financed. On the contrary. Buffett said:

"I asked him to spell his name in lowercase letters so
that everyone would realize that he was the Buffett
without the capital."¹³⁰

~

This little item was found in an *Outstanding Investor*
Digest interview with Buffett's friend, superinvestor
Walter Schloss.

"We understand that Peter Kiewit . . . had a father
who felt the same way as Buffett does about the evils
of inherited wealth," said the interviewer.

"As we recall, much to Peter Kiewit Jr.'s surprise
some years after his father's death, he received a
delayed, out-of-the-blue inheritance of a few million
dollars. While it was peanuts compared to the estate
his father had built and relative to the success he himself achieved, he said it made him feel like his father
was extending his approval from the grave."¹³¹

NOTE: Until Peter Kiewit's death, he was Omaha's
wealthiest and most prominent citizen. Buffett's
offices are in Kiewit Plaza.

~ ✳ ~

WHAT OTHERS SAY
ABOUT WARREN BUFFETT

SUSAN BUFFETT (MAMMA), WARREN'S WIFE

Although Susan and Warren Buffett are not divorced, Mrs. Buffett has lived in San Francisco for nearly two decades. Susie is the mother of the couple's three grown children; she is a major Berkshire Hathaway shareholder in her own right and heir to the Buffett fortune.

When presented with an article by a fan called "Value Investing, the Key to Warren Buffett's Success," Susie Buffett allowed herself to be drawn into light-hearted bantering. When it was suggested that *she* is the key to her husband's success she laughingly agreed.[132] Susie Buffett clearly was joking, but friends, family, and Buffett himself say there is a lot of truth to that.

Of her husband she says: "He's like a color TV instead of a black and white. Most people come in black and white."[133]

Buffett has a little sign on his wall that his wife gave him. It reads:

"A fool and his money are soon invited everywhere."

ASTRID MENKS, BUFFETT'S LIVE-IN COMPANION

Neither Astrid Menks nor Buffett discuss their relationship much, though Buffett admits the triangular arrangement is unusual.

"If you knew everybody well, you'd understand it quite well,"[134] Buffett said.

Menks says: "I have the best of all worlds, and I wouldn't change anything."

As to a reporter who attempted to demean her by referring to her as a "former waitress" or "supper club hostess," she is reported to have replied: "Look, I don't want to be lumped in with those kinds of women. I've been with Warren for 13 years (since 1978). I'm no bimbo and I'm no airhead."[135]

NOTE: There is some question about the accuracy of this quote. Menks apparently was baited into a response by a reporter and the story that followed did not reflect her feelings. She says that, in fact, she respects waitresses, just as she would any other woman working for a living.

SUSAN BUFFETT (LITTLE SUSIE), WARREN'S DAUGHTER

Susie-the-younger is very close to her father, but says she is frustrated by the public perception that she is a wealthy woman. Buffett has always said he wanted to help his children but not help them too much. Especially disturbing to her, Susie says, is the large number of people who ask her for charitable donations.

"They don't understand that when I write my dad a check for $20, he cashes it. If I had $2,000 now, I'd pay off my credit card bill."[136]

NOTE: Buffett now contributes $500,000 a year to a Sherwood Foundation so that each of his children and his companion Astrid Menks can make contributions of their own totalling $100,000 a year or so. Buffett does not check how contributions are made.

~

Growing up, Susie was unaware that her father was atypical: "For years I didn't even know what he did. They asked me at school what he did, and I said he was a security analyst, and they thought he checked alarm systems."[137]

~

Susie knows now, but her father hasn't changed much: "What makes my dad happy is hanging around the house, reading, playing bridge and talking with us. He's about as normal as you can get."[138]

~

"The whole thing is a big game to him. Dollars are the mark of the winner. He doesn't spend anything. He'll drive his car and wear his clothes until they fall apart," young Susie explains.[139]

PETER BUFFETT, WARREN'S SON

Buffett's third and youngest child, Peter, is a successful composer of electronic music. He has written scores for the movies *Dances with Wolves* and *The Scarlet Letter*. Peter, along with his older brother and sister, attended public school in Omaha.

"For as long as I can remember, he thought all three of us should do what made us happy," Peter said of his father. "He was great in that way."

Today, young Buffett says, "He is, essentially, the same guy he was 30 years ago. He'll ask me, 'What do you get paid for something like *The Scarlet Letter?*' 'Well, I got this or that,' and he'll be like, 'Wow, that's a lot of money!'"[140]

~

Peter believes his father's unpretentious ways account for his popularity: "I think that's why he gets the kind of respect that he does. He really has done it honestly and quietly and with a lot of respect for other people."[141]

~

Yet: "My dad says the money is not important, but it is. Not because he wants to spend it, but because it declares him a winner," says Peter Buffett.[142]

LEILA BUFFETT, WARREN'S MOTHER

In junior high school Buffett wasn't a top scholar, though his mother said his poor grades were only temporary: "I think Warren was just going through a phase at the time. He always got very good grades before and after that. He was a good boy. Easy to raise. He never gave us any trouble at all. He never smoked or drank."[143]

When asked if she knew her son would someday accumulate so much wealth: "Ohmy, no; I never dreamed that would happen. But Warren always had a fascination for numbers in connection with earning money."[144]

~

His mother valued Buffett for himself rather than his wealth: "I'm more proud of him for the kind of human being he has become. He's a wonderful person."[145]

NOTE: Leila Buffett passed away in the summer of 1996.

"Doc" William Angle

Doc Angle was one of Omaha's "Buffett millionaires." An early investor, he placed just over $10,000 with Buffett in the 1950s. By the early 1990s, that investment had grown to more than $100 million. Angle died several years ago but his family still owns shares.

"Warren may seem easygoing, but nothing upsets him like losing money—he loves winning. He loves the game. The end is always the money—not to spend it of course, but to accumulate it."[146]

Walter Schloss

Buffett was at Columbia University when he met Walter Schloss. Later, the two worked together at Graham-Newman Co. Schloss then left to open his own investment firm. Buffett has called him a "superinvestor of Graham & Doddsville." Schloss recalled the young Buffett:

"One of the reasons why Warren is such an attractive personality is that he has such a great sense of humor and all those terrific stories. But apparently he was shy when he was young and decided that he wanted to overcome it. So he went to the Dale Carnegie course. . . .

"I saw him in Omaha back in 1961 or 1962 when he got up before a Rotary Club and gave a brilliant speech culminating in asking for money. He was the youngest person, there and it was very, very funny. I wish I had a tape recorder. It was great."[147]

~

As to the high share price of Berkshire Hathaway stock, Schloss says it's far better to multiply the number of Berkshire shares outstanding by the share price, then compare that to other companies of similar size in terms of revenues and assets.

"People do not take into consideration the market value of a company they're buying. They just look at the price per share rather than the value of the company."[148]

NOTE: For more on Schloss, see page 101.

PHIL CARRET

Carret is one of the successful long-term investors described by John Train in *The New Money Masters*. Though he is 99 years old, Carret never misses Berkshire's annual meeting. Of Buffett, he says:

"He's a friend of mine. He's smarter than I am. He proved that in General Foods. It was a stodgy company, mostly coffee. When Berkshire Hathaway bought the stock, I said to myself, 'Well, Warren's made a mistake this time; it was about $60 when I noticed the transaction. In a matter of months, it went to $120 . . . ha, ha!' (Carret has a deep, throaty chuckle when he tells stories of this sort. He particularly enjoys tales describing common opinions that are completely mistaken.)"[149]

BILL GATES, FOUNDER OF MICROSOFT

Gates' mother invited him to a day-long picnic, where she planned to introduce her son to Buffett, his rival as the wealthiest person in America. Gates balked, thinking he had little to say to a man who did nothing but invest all day long. He decided to go when he heard that Katharine Graham, former publisher of *The Washington Post*, also would attend.

When Gates and Buffett met, however, they fell into conversation and soon became buddies. Buffett attended Gates' wedding in Hawaii; later, Warren and Susan Buffett joined him on a tour of China. Though Gates describes their talks as "candid and not at all adversarial," they do "joust now and then" over mathematics.

Gates says Buffett once challenged him to a game of dice, using a set of four unusual dice with a combination of numbers from 0 to 12 on the sides. Buffett suggested that each of them choose one of the die, then discard the other two. They would bet on who would roll the highest number most often. Buffett said Gates could pick his die first. This suggestion instantly roused Gates' curiosity. He asked to examine the dice, after which he demanded that Buffett choose first.

"It wasn't immediately evident that because of the clever selection of numbers for the dice they were nontransitive," Gates said. "The mathematical principle of transivity, that if A beats B and B beats C, then A beats C, did not apply. Assuming ties were rerolled, each of the four dice could be beaten by one of the others: Die A would beat B an average of 11 out of every 17 rolls—almost two-thirds of the time. Die B would beat C with the same frequency. Likewise, C would beat D 11/17 of the time too. And improbable as it sounds, die D would beat A just as often."[150]

JOHN TRAIN,
AUTHOR OF THE NEW MONEY MASTERS
"Professionally, he is in the vulture business, but he is a cheerful sort of vulture." [151]

JACK BYRNE, CHAIRMAN OF GEICO

Byrne and a group of golfing buddies were on an outing at Pebble Beach, when the group playfully offered Buffett a bet: his $10 against their $20,000 that he couldn't score a hole in one over the next three days. Everyone agreed to the wager but Buffett.

"Well, we heaped abuse on him and tried to cajole him—after all it was only $10," Byrne said. "But he said he thought it over and decided it wasn't a good bet for him. He said if you let yourself be undisciplined on the small things, you'd probably be undisciplined on the large things too."[152]

MICHAEL A. GOLDBERG, WHO OPERATES
BERKSHIRE HATHAWAY'S INSURANCE BUSINESS

"Warren Buffett is a person who, the closer he gets, the more extraordinary he gets. If you tell people about him, the way he is, they just think you were bamboozled."[153]

~

"He is constantly examining all that he hears: 'Is it consistent and plausible? Is it wrong?' He has a model in his head of the whole world. The computer there compares every new fact with all that he has ever experienced and knows about, and says, 'What does this mean for us?'"[154]

WRITER LALLY WEYMOUTH
(AND DAUGHTER OF KATHERINE GRAHAM)

"I think the secret of his success is his undiminished curiosity."[155]

CHUCK HUGGINS, HEAD OF SEE'S CANDY

"When I talk to him, he's always up, always positive."[156]

OHIO CONGRESSMAN DENNIS ECKART

At a 1991 Congressional hearing on the Salomon government securities trading incident, Eckhart applauded Buffett for taking responsibility: "Gordon Gekko and Sherman McCoy are alive and well on Wall Street. Mr. Buffett, get in there and kick some butt."[157]

IRVING KAHN,
NEW YORK INVESTMENT MANAGER

Kahn served for many years as Ben Graham's classroom assistant at Columbia University. He first met Buffett there. "He was much the same as he is now, but he was a brash, cocky young guy—he was always busy on his own. He has tremendous energy. He could wear you out talking to you. He was very ambitious about making money."[158]

ACTRESS SWOOZIE KURTZ,
DISTANT RELATIVE AND FRIEND

"People still think Warren is this bumpkin from Omaha. And he'd just as soon let them think that. But nothing could be further from the truth. He's an enormously sophisticated man."[159]

ANTHONY ABBOTT,
OWNER OF THE FRENCH CAFE, OMAHA

Maybe, Abbott suggests, we get the Warren Buffett we demand: "Warren is a hero, and people like their myths neat and uncomplicated. Of course, none of this is uncomplicated."[160]

WORK THINGS OUT
WITH YOUR WIFE

Outsiders, and in some cases friends and family, don't understand why Warren and Susan Buffett remain married but live apart. Yet those who spend time around the Buffetts and get to know Buffett's companion Astrid Menks sense that there are no victims in the arrangement. Buffett, who speaks tenderly of his wife, once described Susie Buffett this way: "She sort of roams. She's a free spirit."[161]

~

Around the time her youngest child was graduating from high school, Susie Buffett launched a nightclub singing career. She told a reporter: "I'm really proud of myself. Because there's nothing I would be more vulnerable about trying than singing. Nothing. I'm so proud that I did it. I can't believe I did."[162]

~

Her husband, Susie says, encouraged her: "It was Warren. He's the one. He knew. He said to me, 'Susie, you're like somebody who has lost his job after 23 years. Now what are you going to do?' He knew I wanted to sing. But I was scared to death."

And what was Buffett's motive? "Warren understands me. And he wants me to stay alive. If you love someone, you do."[163]

~

Family friend Eunice Denenberg sees Mrs. Buffett this way: "Susie is one of those old-fashioned *good* people that lots of folks today don't think exist. So they attribute some of their own baser behavior to her because it bothers them."[164]

BE KIND TO YOUR MOTHER

Some authors have described Buffett's mother as moody and difficult to grow up with. Buffett speaks affectionately of her. He was generous with the 92-year-old widow and sometimes introduced her at annual meetings. He once bought himself an exercise bike, and bought one (along with a new car) for his mom:

"Between the two of us, we put 25,000 miles on those machines. But all the mileage was on hers . . . I should have bought her a bicycle, instead of a Cadillac."[165]

~

Buffett's mother shed more light on the situation: "Warren gave me a Cadillac for my 80th birthday. I've got only 8,000 miles on it. But I've put 19,190 miles on my Exercycle."[166]

~

Likewise, Buffett appreciates the gifts his mother gave to him:

"My health is terrific. I just went for the first time in six or seven years for a general checkup. The doctor asked me about my diet and said, 'You're counting rather heavily on your genes, aren't you?'"[167]

~ ✳ ~

WHAT THE CRITICS SAY

Despite his reputation as a straight shooter, Buffett has critics. *The Wall Street Journal* accused him of taking advantage of his reputation and wealth to secure deals that other investors cannot get.

"By offering help against takeover attacks to USAir, Gillette, and Salomon, he has managed to extract exclusive and highly favorable investment deals for his Berkshire Hathaway investment company that weren't available to other shareholders; these three deals alone total $1.7 billion."

And later in the same story, "Mr. Buffett has 'done a bril-liant job of convincing people' that his white squire invest-ments are good for America, says a well-known raider. But the jury is still out on whether the companies are being smart in forging protection arrangements with Mr. Buffett."[168]

NOTE: Buffett later was forced to take a management role at Salomon to help the company recover from an episode of illegal government bond trading; he also had to take a write-down of $268.5 million on the USAir investment. Buffett began pulling out of those two companies when the opportunity arose. Gillette, however, has done well. Ultimately, Berkshire Hathaway did not actually experience a loss on USAir. Not only did the shares return to the price Buffett paid for them, USAir declared a substantial dividend.

SIR JAMES GOLDSMITH, BRITISH INDUSTRIALIST

"I don't understand people like Warren Buffett who pride themselves on living in their first house and driving a used Chevy to work, despite being billionaires."

After that quote ran in *Time* magazine, Goldsmith called Buffett and apologized, implying that he was misquoted.[169]

ALLEN GREENE, COPY EDITOR AND LATER, UNION PRESIDENT, THE BUFFALO NEWS

When asked in 1982 if *The Buffalo News* could initiate a profit-sharing plan, considering its high profitability, Buffett is said to have replied: "There's nothing you people on the third floor (the newsroom) do that has any effect on my profits, so I don't feel any desire to share them with you."

Greene said of *The Buffalo News* staff, "We were stunned. We thought he was such a nice guy."[170]

NOTE: Stan Lipsey, publisher of *The Buffalo News* says he was present at all meetings Buffett had with union members, and he does not remember Buffett making this comment. Buffett may have made a general statement about the economics of newspapers that dominate a market, which may have been interpreted this way by Greene, Lipsey says. Greene stands behind his statement.

MICHAEL LEWIS, AUTHOR

Not everyone thinks Buffett is a genius, and former Salomon trader and author of *Liar's Poker* Michael Lewis seems to be one of them: "He regularly ridicules skeptical professors with a vaguely thuggish if-you're-so-smart-why-am-I-rich routine. (The reason he is rich is simply that random games produce big winners, but pity the business school professor on $50 grand a year who tries to argue with a billionaire.)"[171]

ABOUT WORK

Philosophers tell us to do what we love and success will follow. Buffett is living proof that it works.

WORK FOR THE FUN OF IT

Warren Buffett noted that when he graduated from Columbia:

> *"Wall Street (in 1951) wasn't a hot place to work at all. The Dow was 200, and the market from 1945 to 1949 had gone sort of sideways. The high was about 190 and the low was about 160. Then it started moving up; 1950 was the first year the Dow never sold below 200. In 1929, it sold at 381, but during the year it was below 200. So people were very suspicious about the postwar (era) and thought we were going into a depression. (Wall Street) was not a big money place to work . . . it was quite a different world."*[172]

Buffett says working with people you don't like is like "marrying for money":

"I think that's kind of a crazy way to live. It's probably a bad idea under any circumstances, but absolutely nuts if you're already rich."[173]

~

"What I am is a realist. *I always knew I'd like what I'm doing. Oh, perhaps it would have been nice to be a major league baseball player, but that's where the realism comes in."*[174]

~

"It's not that I want *money. It's the fun of making money and watching it grow."*[175]

~

"I'm the luckiest guy in the world in terms of what I do for a living. No one can tell me to do things I don't believe in or things I think are stupid."[176]

~

Buffett is often encouraged to run for political office:

"I wouldn't trade my job for any job, and that includes political life."[177]

~

Buffett describes Berkshire Hathaway as "my canvas."[178]

"I have a blank canvas and a lot of paint, and I get to do what I want. Now there is more money

*and things are on a bigger scale, but I had just
as much fun 10 or 20 years ago when it was on a
smaller scale.*"[179]

~

*"When I go to my office every morning, I feel like
I'm going to the Sistine Chapel to paint."*[180]

~

*"(I) enjoy the process far more than the proceeds,
though (I) have learned to live with those also."*[181]

~

Buffett's maternal grandfather owned a newspaper, and
Warren earned much of his early income as a carrier
for *The Washington Post* and as circulation manager
for the *Lincoln Journal*. Newspapers are in his blood:

*"Let's face it, newspapers are a hell of a lot more
interesting business than, say, making couplers for
rail cars. While I don't get involved in the editorial
operations of the papers I own, I really enjoy being
part of the institutions that help shape society."*[182]

~

*"My guess is that if Ted Williams was getting the
highest salary in baseball and he was hitting .220,
he would be unhappy. And if he was getting the
lowest salary in baseball and batting .400, he'd be
very happy. That's the way I feel about doing this*

job. Money is a by-product of doing something I like doing extremely well."[183]

～

"I feel like tap dancing all the time."[184]

START EARLY

Buffett bought his first stock at age 11 when he and his sister Doris bought three shares of Cities Service preferred stock for $38 per share. He also learned a lesson about patience. When the stock fell to $27, they became a little concerned. After Cities Service rallied to $40, they sold the shares but the stock price kept going—eventually climbing to $200 per share.

～

"I'd been interested in the stock market from the time I was 11, when I spent some time watching the market and marking the board at Harris Upham, a New York Stock Exchange firm that was in the same building as my dad's firm, Buffett-Falk & Co."[185]

～

Throughout his childhood, Buffett got involved in many businesses. He sold Cokes at a markup to his friends, published a race track tip sheet, carried newspapers, and recycled golf balls. While at Woodrow Wilson High School in Washington, he and a friend bought a reconditioned pinball machine for $25. Operating as the Wilson Coin Operated Machine Company, they put the game in a barbershop. They checked the coin box at the end of the first day and found $4. "I figured I had discovered the wheel," Buffett said.[186]

Eventually, the pinball business was netting $50 per week. Later, Buffett bought an unimproved farm in northeastern Nebraska and had $9,000 in the bank by the time he graduated from high school.[187]

～

Buffett developed an early reputation as an investor:

"I shorted a few shares of American Telephone because I knew that all my (high school) teachers owned it. They thought I knew about stocks, and I thought if I shorted AT&T, I would terrorize them about their retirement."[188]

WORK WHERE YOU WANT TO WORK

When asked why he forgoes working in New York where he could be nearer the financial markets and the rumor mill, Buffett replied:

"With enough inside information and a million dollars, you can go broke in a year."[189]

～

"I probably have more friends in New York and California than here, but this is a good place to bring up children and a good place to live. You can think here. You can think better about the market; you don't hear so many stories, and you can just sit and look at the stock on the desk in front of you. You can think about a lot of things."[190]

~

But he also says:

"If a graduating MBA were to ask me, 'How do I get rich in a hurry?' I would not respond with quotations from Ben Franklin or Horatio Alger, but would instead hold my nose with one hand and point with the other toward Wall Street."[191]

WORK WITH GOOD PEOPLE

"I choose to work with every single person that I work with. That ends up being the most important factor. I don't interact with people I don't like or admire. That's the key. It's like marrying."[192]

~

"I work with sensational people, and I do what I want in life. Why shouldn't I? If I'm not in a position to do what I want, who the hell is?"[193]

~

"Somebody once said that in looking for people to hire, you look for three qualities: integrity, intelli-

gence, and energy. And if they don't have the first, the other two will kill you. You think about it; it's true. If you hire somebody without the first, you really want them to be dumb and lazy."[194]

∼

When a graduate student sought job counseling, Buffett said:

"I believe in going to work for businesses you admire and people you admire. Anytime you're around somebody that you're getting something out of and you feel good about the organization, you just have to get a good result. I advise you never to do anything because you think it's miserable now but it's going to be great 10 years from now, or because you think I've got X dollars now, but I'll have 10X. If you're not enjoying it today, you're probably not going to enjoy it 10 years from now."[195]

∼

Who you work for makes a big difference. Buffett remembers that, at one time, players like Babe Ruth and Lou Gehrig voted a full share of their World Series proceeds to their bat boy:

"The key in life is to figure out who to be the bat boy for."[196]

∼

Buffett admits that his advice to college students has had unexpected outcomes:

"I gave a talk last year; some student at Harvard asked me, 'Who should I go to work for?' I said go to work for whoever you admire the most. I got a call from the dean about two weeks later. He said, 'What are you telling these kids? They're all becoming self-employed.'"[197]

NOTE: A gentle get-back there? Buffett applied to Harvard before he was admitted to Columbia, but Harvard rejected him. But Buffett seems to hold no grudge. The only brand-new MBA he ever hired was a young woman from Harvard.

GIVE A PAT ON THE BACK

Buffett wrote to Katharine Graham of *The Washington Post* in 1984:

"Berkshire Hathaway bought its shares in The Washington Post *in the spring and summer of 1973. The cost of these shares was $10.6 million, and the present market value is about $140 million. . . . If we had spent this same $10.6 million at the same time in the shares of . . . other (media companies) . . . we now would have either $50 million worth of Dow Jones, $30 million worth of Gannett, $75 million worth of Knight-Ridder, $60 million worth of* The New York Times, *or $40 million of Times Mirror. So, instead of thanks a million, make it thanks anywhere from $65 to $110 million."*[198]

BE LOYAL TO YOUR PARTNERS

Buffett acknowledges that money and power could give him undue advantage over partners, employees, and others:

> *"One time we had a dog on our roof, and my son called to him and he jumped. He lived, but he broke a leg. It was awful. The dog that loves you so much that he jumps off the roof ... you can put people into those situations too. I don't want to do that."*[199]

When Berkshire Hathaway invested in Cap Cities/ABC, Buffett promised Chairman Tom Murphy that it would be for the long term, even if the company's television network problems were not quickly resolved:

> *"It's like if you have a kid that has problems: it's not something we're going to sell in five years. We're partners in it."*[200]

> *"We're not pure economic creatures, and that policy penalizes our results somewhat, but we prefer to operate that way in life. What's the sense of becoming rich if you're going to have a pattern of operation where you continually discard associations with people you like, admire, and find interesting in order to earn a slightly bigger figure? We like big figures, but not to the exclusion of everything else."*[201]

"I don't think I would feel good about myself if I went around dumping people after they trusted me."[202]

GUARD YOUR TIME

Warren's oldest son Howard eventually came to understand his father's time management process: "My father couldn't run a lawnmower . . . I never saw him cut the grass, trim a hedge, or wash a car. I remember that used to be irritating, and only when I got older and understood the value of time did I realize why he did things the way he did. His time is so valuable."[203]

~

"It's not a plus to get terribly well known," says Warren Buffett. "As you can see (waving toward the small suite that makes up Berkshire Hathaway headquarters), we are not equipped to handle tons of inquiries. We get letters from people all over who want advice on investments. I don't like to be hard-nosed, but there's also no way I can do it and get my job done."[204]

~

Buffett rarely gives speeches or makes public appearances on behalf of civic or business organizations. He makes about a dozen speeches, mostly question-and-answer sessions, at universities each year.

"If you talk to 100 students and you say something

that makes sense, a few of them may pay attention to it, and it may actually change their lives, as opposed to a bunch of 60-year-olds." Buffett, who was 63 at the time, apparently knows this from experience. "I mean, I can go hear a speech and I know whether I'm entertained or not, but I probably won't change anything I do."[205]

~

Buffett borrowed his time-management principles from a pro:

> *"Well, I just use the Nancy Reagan policy. I just say no."*[206]

KNOW WHEN TO QUIT

> *"That which is not worth doing is not worth doing well."*[207]

~

> *"If at first you do succeed, quit trying."*[208]

~

In 1969, when the stock market was on a high, Buffett took early retirement. He shut down the Buffett Partnership, which had experienced a thirty-fold increase in value, and returned the money to investors. He was 38 years old:

> *"I don't want to be totally occupied with outpacing an investment rabbit all my life."*

He added:

"I have no urge to keep piling up money."

And finally:

"The only way to slow down is to stop."[209]

NOTE: He didn't stay away from work long. Buffett was soon creating his new investment vehicle, Berkshire Hathaway, from the cloth of a textile manufacturing concern.

ABOUT RUNNING A BUSINESS

COMMUNICATE WELL

How does Buffett write such clear and candid annual reports, especially since they have no graphs or photos? Write it for someone you know.

> *"I just assume my sister owns the other half of the business and she's been traveling for a year. She's not business-ignorant, but she's not an expert, either. I don't see anything wrong with graphics. It's just that I think there is a tendency when people emphasize, to deemphasize real information."*[210]

> *"If you understand an idea, you can express it so others can understand it. I find that every year when I write the report. I hit these blocks. The block isn't because I've run out of words in the dictionary. The block is because I haven't got it straight in my own mind yet. There's nothing like writing to force you to think and to get your thoughts straight."*[211]

Berkshire's high share price is one way of communicating to people that Buffett wants serious investors who acquire the shares for the long term. He wants people to know what they're getting into:

"We could stick a sign outside this hall tonight and put 'rock concert' on it, and we'd have one kind of crowd come in. And we could put 'ballet' and we'd have a somewhat different kind of crowd come in. Both crowds are fine. But it's a terrible mistake to put rock concert out there if you're going to have a ballet, or vice versa. And the only way I have of sticking a sign on Berkshire, as to the kind of place I'm asking people to enter, is through the communications and policies."[212]

KNOW WHEN TO SAY NO

When asked to comment on the 1992 purchase of shares in Wells Fargo & Co., a woman answering the telephone at Berkshire gave the company's standard reply: "It has long been the policy at Berkshire Hathaway that we never comment on our portfolio or rumors about our portfolio."[213]

~

There is a reason for Buffett's silence on investment activities:

"If I say anything, I know it (the low price that interests him) will be gone. You can't telegraph your punches in a financial situation."[214]

~

When Buffett wants to send a warning shot across the bow, he is capable of expressing himself succinctly. Such was the case when he worked with Salomon to resolve its government securities trading improprieties:

"We (Salomon) will pay any fines or penalties with dispatch, and we will also try to settle valid legal claims promptly. However, we will litigate invalid or inflated claims, of which there will be many, to whatever extent necessary. That is, we will make appropriate amends for past conduct but we will be no one's patsy."[215]

SET AN EXAMPLE

During his stint as interim chairman of Salomon Inc., Buffett told shareholders:

"An atmosphere encouraging exemplary behavior is probably even more important than rules, necessary though they are. During my tenure as chairman, I will consider myself the firm's chief compliance officer, and I have asked all 9,000 of Salomon's employees to assist me in that effort. I have also urged them to be guided by a test that goes beyond rules. Contemplating any business act, an employee should ask himself whether he would be willing to see it immediately described by an informed and critical reporter on the front page of his local

paper, there to be read by his spouse, children, and friends. At Salomon, we simply want no part of any activities that pass legal tests but that we, as citizens, would find offensive."[216]

TAKE CARE OF SHAREHOLDERS

Berkshire Hathaway investor Gerald L. "Bud" Pearson says he heard about Buffett from a friend in 1965. Pearson went to talk to Buffett, who told him that he'd stopped accepting new investors to his partnership. After talking to Pearson for an hour, Buffett changed his mind.

"Aw, heck, you seem like a nice guy," Buffett said. In time, Pearson became a "Buffett millionaire."[217]

～

When asked why thousands of shareholders travel long distances to attend Berkshire Hathaway's annual meeting in Omaha each year, Buffett surmised:

"They come because we make them feel like owners."[218]

～

Buffett likes to invest in businesses where managers think like owners. He tried to shift the corporate culture at Salomon:

"We wish to see the unit's managers become wealthy through ownership, not by simply free-riding on

the ownership of others, I think, in fact, that owner-ship can in time bring our best managers substantial wealth, perhaps in amounts well beyond what they now think possible."[219]

As of this writing, Buffett's plan was meeting limited success at Salomon. When the time came to start converting Berkshire's preferred shares into Salomon common stock, Buffett declined the option. It is possible that his decision had some connection to employee attitudes regarding compensation.

∼

Salomon bond trader Paul Mozer was charged with illegal treasury securities trading, allegedly in an attempt to corner the market. The incident posed a serious threat to the survival of the entire company. Buffett observed: "Mozer's paying $30,000 and is sentenced to prison for four months. Salomon's shareholders—including me—paid $290 million, and I got sentenced to ten months as CEO."[220]

HIRE WELL, MANAGE LITTLE

Buffett says his employment form has one question:

"Are you a fanatic?"

The best investors are.[221]

∼

"I like guys who forget that they sold the business to me and run the show like proprietors. When I marry the daughter, she continues to live with her parents."

$\sim$

Buffett expects his managers to be just that:

"If they need my help to manage the enterprise, we're probably both in trouble."[222]

Exceptions: Each year, Buffett sets prices on See's Candy and circulation rates for *The Buffalo News*. Both management and Buffett say that because he's some distance from the operations, he has greater objectivity.

PUT A PREMIUM ON EXPERIENCE

"Can you really explain to a fish what it's like to walk on land? One day on land is worth a thousand years of talking about it, and one day running a business has exactly the same kind of value."[223]

BE SMART ABOUT ALLOCATING CAPITAL

An advantage of owning a company outright, rather than simply holding shares, is the ability to reinvest profits efficiently, even if that means moving funds to a different industry:

"We're not in the steel business, per se. We're not in the shoe business, per se. We're not in any business,

per se. We're big in insurance, but we're not commit-
ted to it. We don't have a mind-set that says you have
to go down this road. So we can take capital and
move it into businesses that make sense."[224]

BE BRAVE

After he finished college, Buffett invested $100 in a
Dale Carnegie course:

". . . not to prevent my knees from knocking when
public speaking but to do public speaking while my
knees were knocking."[225]

USE CROSSOVER SKILLS

"I am a better investor because I am a businessman,
and a better businessman because I am an investor."[226]

～

"I feel the same way about managing that I do
about investing: It's just not necessary to do extraor-
dinary things to get extraordinary results."[227]

～ ＊ ～

THE BERKSHIRE HATHAWAY
ANNUAL MEETING

Thousands of investors and admirers descend upon
Omaha each spring to sit in a crowded meeting hall for
hours to hear what Warren Buffett has to say. He stays
until all questions are answered, and if the questions

are still rolling in when lunchtime comes, shareholders can go to the lobby to buy sandwiches and a Coca-Cola. Every year, Buffett sets down the rules by which the annual meeting will be conducted. These examples are collected from several different years:

> *"The business of the meeting will be handled in our usual Stalinistic manner to allow plenty of time to answer shareholder's questions."*[228]

> ∿

> *"If you must leave during the meeting, it's better form to leave while Charlie's talking—which is rarely."*[229]

> ∿

> *"I'd like to introduce Berkshire's managers, except Mrs. B couldn't take time off from work for foolishness like a shareholders' meeting."*[230]

> ∿

> *"We'll be here to answer questions until around noon or until Charlie says something optimistic, whichever comes first."*[231]

> ∿

> *"After the meeting, there will be buses to take out-of-town guests to the Nebraska Furniture Mart, Borsheim's jewelry, or anyplace else that Berkshire has an economic interest in."*[232]

The preceding is no joke. In the lobby of the meeting hall there are carts selling See's Candy, Ginzu knives, World Book encyclopedias and other Berkshire Hathaway-owned products. The trips to the Berkshire Hathaway-owned stores are not only so people can shop, but also to serve an educational purpose, Buffett insists. One must: "go to the Nebraska Furniture Mart and see Mrs. B in her natural setting."[233]

~

Charlie Munger occasionally makes a marketing pitch of his own. He especially likes World Book encyclopedias: "I give away more of that product than any other product that Berkshire Hathaway makes . . . . it's a perfectly fabulous human achievement. To edit something that user-friendly with that much wisdom encapsulated is a fabulous thing."[234]

~

While serving as interim chairman, Buffett presided over the 1992 Salomon Brothers annual meeting. It lasted three hours, as Buffett faced a grilling from shareholders who wanted more information about Salomon's government bond-trading offenses. Berkshire Hathaway held a major investment in Salomon, and Buffett was working without salary to restore the company's credibility in the market after a trader allegedly attempted to illegally corner a dominant position in U.S. Treasury bonds. Famous gadfly shareholder Evelyn Y. Davis asked Buffett how he could justify charging $158,000 for the cost of his corporate jet, which shuttled Buffett between Omaha and New York City. Buffett replied:

"I work cheap, but I travel expensive."

Davis also groused about the $25 million in lawyer's fees associated with the resolution of Salomon's problems:

"I would be delighted to have you negotiate with them, Evelyn. And I think the mere mention of that would be enough to induce a little moderation."[235]

As more people become Berkshire shareholders, logistics for the annual meeting get trickier:

"Most of you know we held our annual meeting at the Joslyn Art Museum the past several years until we outgrew it. Since the Orpheum Theater, where we're meeting today, is an old vaudeville theater, I suppose we've slid down the cultural chain. Don't ask me where we'll go next."

In 1995, the meeting moved to the convention center at the Holiday Inn and, again, the hall was packed. Berkshire's shareholder base doubled in 1996 with the issuance of the Berkshire B shares, but the Holiday Inn is Omaha's largest indoor venue. The racetrack in 1997?

Linda O'Bryon asked about the meeting on the Nightly Business Report.

"We'll have to come up with an answer and I'm a little bit like Scarlet O'Hara on that. I think I'll worry about that tomorrow," Buffett said. [236]

ABOUT INVESTING

Warren Buffett employs investment principles that he describes as "simple, old, and few."[237] Many of Buffett's methods evolve from his personality and character. Others he has learned from teachers and experience. Like all good students, he uses his training as a foundation. In time, he stacked the bricks far higher than his best teachers.

HAVE A PHILOSOPHY

"Rule No. 1: Never lose money. Rule No. 2: Never forget Rule No. 1."[238]

~

Buffett returns again and again to Ben Graham:

"I consider there to be three basic ideas, ideas that if they are really ground into your intellectual framework, I don't see how you could help but do reasonably well in stocks. None of them are complicated. None of them take mathematical talent or anything

*of the sort. (Graham) said you should look at stocks
as small pieces of the business. Look at (market)
fluctuations as your friend rather than your enemy—
profit from folly rather than participate in it. And in
(the last chapter of* The Intelligent Investor*), he
said the three most important words of investing:
'margin of safety.' I think those ideas, 100 years from
now, will still be regarded as the three cornerstones
of sound investing."*[239]

Buffett summarizes Graham this way:

*"When proper temperament joins with proper intel-
lectual framework, then you get rational behavior."*[240]

Buffett is not concerned about his principles going stale:

*"If principles can become dated, they're not prin-
ciples."*[241]

RECOGNIZE THE ENEMY: INFLATION

*"The arithmetic makes it plain that inflation is a far
more devastating tax than anything that has been
enacted by our legislature. The inflation tax has a
fantastic ability to simply consume capital. It makes
no difference to a widow with her savings in a 5 percent passbook account whether she pays 100 percent
income tax on her interest income during a period of
zero inflation, or pays no income taxes during years*

of 5 percent inflation. Either way, she is 'taxed' in a manner that leaves her no real income whatsoever. Any money she spends comes right out of capital. She would find outrageous a 120 percent income tax, but doesn't seem to notice that 5 percent inflation is the economic equivalent."[242]

~

"If you feel you can dance in and out of securities in a way that defeats the inflation tax, I would like to be your broker—but not your partner."[243]

~

Buffett explains why he holds stocks even in times of high inflation: "Partly it's habit. Partly, it's just that stocks mean business, and owning businesses is much more interesting than owning gold or farmland. Besides, stocks are probably still the best of all the poor alternatives in an era of inflation—at least they are if you buy in at appropriate prices."[244]

~

Buffett has a few ideas on how to control inflation:

"I could eliminate inflation or reduce it very easily, if you had a constitutional amendment that said that no congressman or senator was eligible for reelection in a year in which the CPI increased more than over 3 percent."[245]

~

EXPERIENCE EPIPHANY

Buffett was 19 years old and a senior at the University of Nebraska when he read Graham's classic *The Intelligent Investor*. He likens the experience to that of "Paul on the road to Damascus," and one in which he learned the philosophy of "buying $1 for 40 cents."[246]

Before reading the book, Buffett says, "I went the whole gamut. I collected charts and I read all the technical stuff. I listened to tips. And then I picked up Graham's *The Intelligent Investor*. That was like seeing the light.[247]

"I don't want to sound like a religious fanatic or anything, but it really did get me."[248]

~

"Prior to that, I had been investing with my glands instead of my head."[249]

~ ✳ ~

BENJAMIN GRAHAM

Warren Buffett first became acquainted with Graham when he read his book, *The Intelligent Investor*. He met his hero in person in 1950 when Buffett enrolled in graduate school at Columbia University: "Next to my dad, Ben Graham had more impact certainly on my business life than any individual," Buffett says.

Graham, he explained, was more interested in the intellectual challenge of investing than in building a fortune. That, along with vast intellectual curiosity, generosity, and a wry sense of humor, made Graham unique.[250]

~

Graham and Buffett had much in common. Articulate and witty, Graham enjoyed a wide circle of friends. The chief similarity is a peculiar (to the rest of us) disinterest in lots of money. Shortly after Buffett joined Graham's firm, Graham told him: "Money won't make any difference to you and me. We won't change. Only our wives will live better."[251]

When Buffett graduated from Columbia in 1951, Graham suggested that he postpone his career in investments until the overheated market took a rest. During that year, the Dow Jones Industrial Average hit 250. Until then, the DJIA had traded at below 200 in every year since its inception.

"I had about 10 thousand bucks," Buffett said. "If I'd taken (the) advice, I'd probably still have about 10 thousand bucks."[252]

It was an uncharacteristic suggestion, since Graham had built a career warning against market timing. Graham retired in 1956, apparently weary of working and no longer interested in stocks.

NOTE: Buffett ended up with much more money than Graham. When Graham died in 1976 at age 82, he left an estate of around $3 million. 🗋

~

"(Graham) wasn't about brilliant investments and he wasn't about fads or fashion. He was about sound investing, and I think sound investing can make you very wealthy if you're not in too big of a hurry. And it never makes you poor, which is better."[253]

~

"It baffles us how many people know of Ben Graham, but so few follow. We tell our principles freely and write about them extensively in our annual reports. They are easy to learn. They should be easy to follow. But the only thing anyone wants to know is, 'what are you buying today?' Like Graham, we are widely recognized but least followed."[254]

~

"Most of us, when we get our ideas about investing, we guard them jealously and don't talk about them until we've bought the last share that we can afford. Then we start shouting. Ben was something else on that. He regularly taught at Columbia or the New York Institute of Finance. He never taught a class without current examples, and he was perfectly willing to share what other people thought of as secrets. It is sort of the ultimate act of generosity when you go out and teach someone something that is actually going to be harmful to your own commercial well-being, and I saw Ben do that." Buffett laughed and added, "That is a part of Ben I didn't carry forward."[255]

NOTE: Buffett does not reveal his purchases until required to do so by the Securities and Exchange Commission, or long after the fact when explaining Berkshire Hathaway's performance to investors. Generally, Berkshire does not announce investments of under $600 million.

~

Here are some typical Graham observations on investing and the markets:

"Pascal said that 'the heart has reasons that reason doesn't understand.' For 'heart' read Wall Street."[256]

～

Though Graham, like Buffett, had an innate love for math, he warned against any investor who bases investments on overly impressive charts, graphs, or formulas: "Even when the underlying motive of a purchaser of a security is mere speculative greed, human nature desires to conceal this unlovely impulse behind a screen of apparent logic and good sense."[257]

～

Graham often reminded investors that they own the companies in which they invest, and as owners, should not let themselves be bullied by management: "I want to say a word about disgruntled shareholders. In my humble opinion, not enough of them are disgruntled. And one of the great troubles with Wall Street is that it cannot distinguish between a mere trouble maker or 'strike suitor' in corporate affairs and a stockholder with a legitimate complaint which deserves attention from his management and from his shareholders."[258]

～

Despite his admiration for Graham, Buffett departs in several notable ways: "Ben Graham wanted everything to be a quantitative bargain. I want it to be a quantitative bargain in terms of future streams of cash. My guess is the last big time to do it Ben's way was in '73 or '74, when you could have done it quite easily."[259]

～

"I'm willing to pay more for a good business and for good management than I would 20 years ago. Ben tended to look at the statistics alone. I've looked more and more at the intangibles."[260]

～

William Ruane, founder of the highly successful Sequoia Fund met Warren Buffett when both attended Graham's seminar at Columbia. Together, he says, Graham and Buffett paint a complete picture of how to invest:

"(Graham) wrote what we call the Bible, and Warren's thinking updated it. Warren wrote the New Testament."[261]

～

In his later years, Graham told Buffett that every day he hoped to do "something foolish, something creative, and something generous." Graham said he usually was able to get the first one accomplished before breakfast.[262]

～

When Graham was in his late 70s and laid ill in a San Diego hospital, he asked Buffett to help him revise *The Intelligent Investor* for a new edition. Buffett agreed, but later Graham recovered and proceeded on his own. Graham seemed not to like the modifications Buffett proposed. What were those changes? Not many, Buffett said: "I wanted to talk a little more about inflation and about how the investor should analyze businesses. But I was not going to change the ten commandments at all."[263]

Graham's theories are seldom included in college curriculums today because, according to Buffett: "It's not difficult enough. So, instead, something is taught that is difficult but not useful. The business schools reward complex behavior more than simple behavior, but simple behavior is more effective."[264]

~

Buffett hears from investors all over the world who share his admiration for Benjamin Graham: "He was true north on a lot of people's compass," Buffett says.[265]

What did Graham have to say about Buffett?

Graham told Del Mar, California investor Charles Brandes, "Warren has done very well."[266]

~ ✳ ~

NEVER MIND WHAT
THE PROFESSORS SAY

Buffett rails against investment theories such as efficient market hypothesis, beta, and other concepts taught today at the major universities. They rely, he believes, too heavily on abstract theory and not enough on common sense:

"I'd be a bum on the street with a tin cup if the markets were always efficient."[267]

~

"Investing in a market where people believe in efficiency is like playing bridge with someone who has been told it doesn't do any good to look at the cards."[268]

~

"It has been helpful to me to have tens of thousands (of students) turned out of business schools taught that it didn't do any good to think."[269]

~

"Current finance classes can help you do average."[270]

~

Buffett's partner Charlie Munger, when asked about modern portfolio theory, instantly replied "Twaddle!" He added that the concepts are "a type of dementia I can't even classify."[271]

~

As for "asset allocation" to the future highest and best-performing industrial group, Buffett also passes:

"For me, it's what's available at the time. We're not interested in categories per se. We're interested in value."[272]

MEET MR. MARKET

Mr. Market was a character invented by Graham to illuminate his students' minds regarding market behavior. The stock market should be viewed as an emotionally disturbed business partner, Graham said. This partner, Mr. Market, shows up each day offering a price at which he will buy your share of the business or sell you his share. No matter how wild his offer is or how often you reject it, Mr. Market returns with a new offer the next day and each day thereafter. Buffett says the moral of the story is this: Mr. Market is your servant, not your guide.

～

In March 1989, as the stock market soared, Buffett wrote:

> *"We have no idea how long the excesses will last, nor do we know what will change the attitudes of the government, lender and buyer that fuel them. But we know that the less prudence with which others conduct their affairs, the greater the prudence with which we should conduct our own affairs."*[273]

～

> *"I never attempt to make money on the stock market. I buy on the assumption that they could close the market the next day and not reopen it for five years."*[274]

～

How can an investor be sure that the price of a stock that is undervalued by the market eventually will rise?

"When I worked for Graham-Newman, I asked Ben Graham, who then was my boss, about that. He just shrugged and replied that the market always eventually does. He was right: in the short run, (the market is) a voting machine; in the long run, it's a weighing machine."[275]

"The fact that people will be full of greed, fear, or folly is predictable. The sequence is not predictable."[276]

"The market, like the Lord, helps those who help themselves."[277]

IGNORE MR. MARKET'S MOODS

"Charlie and I never have an opinion on the market because it wouldn't be any good and it might interfere with the opinions we have that are good."[278]

"You can't get rich with a weather vane."[279]

"The market is there only as a reference point to see if anybody is offering to do anything foolish. When we invest in stocks, we invest in businesses."[280]

"If we find a company we like, the level of the market will not really impact our decisions. We will decide

company by company. We spend essentially no time thinking about macroeconomic factors. In other words, if somebody handed us a prediction by the most revered intellectual on the subject, with figures for unemployment or interest rates, or whatever it might be for the next two years, we would not pay any attention to it. We simply try to focus on businesses that we think we understand and where we like the price and management. If we see anything that relates to what's going to happen in Congress, we don't even read it. We just don't think it's helpful to have a view on these matters."[281]

⌣

"(John Maynard) Keynes essentially said, don't try and figure out what the market is doing. Figure out a business you understand, and concentrate."[282]

⌣

"For some reason, people take their cues from price action rather than from values. What doesn't work is when you start doing things that you don't understand or because they worked last week for somebody else. The dumbest reason in the world to buy a stock is because it's going up."[283]

⌣

"The future is never clear; you pay a very high price in the stock market for a cheery consensus. Uncertainty actually is the friend of the buyer of long-term values."[284]

⌣

LISTEN FOR OPPORTUNITY'S CALL

Though he cannot anticipate market movements, there are times when it is obvious that stock prices in general are too high or too low. The clue is that there are either very few undervalued stocks to buy (the market is in the stratosphere), or there are so many good buys an investor can't take advantage of them all (the market is bottoming). In 1973, stocks were high-priced.

> *"I felt like an oversexed guy on a desert island. I (didn't) find anything to buy."*[285]

In 1974, Buffett's condition didn't change, but his location (like the market) did. He told a reporter:

> *"I feel like an oversexed guy in a harem. This is the time to start investing."*[286]

~

In the spring of 1987, Buffett was asked about the corporate jet he'd purchased, and announced in tiny print in Berkshire's annual report:

> *"I'd rather buy a good stock than a good jet, but there's nothing that we can see buying even if it went down 10 percent."*

He was then asked when the market would decline: "We haven't the faintest idea."

Buffett and the world soon found out. On October, 19, 1987, the Dow Jones Industrial Average fell 507 points in a single day. Before the market correction was over, the Dow lost nearly one-third of its value. In time, the market recovered and surpassed its previous highs.

~

At times Buffett finds no attractive investments:

"Currently liking neither stocks nor bonds, I find myself the polar opposite of Mae West as she declared, 'I only like two kinds of men: foreign and domestic.'"[287]

~

Buffett says he likes to buy stocks when the "bears are giving them away."[288]

KNOW THE DIFFERENCE BETWEEN PRICE AND VALUE

"Price is what you pay. Value is what you get."[289]

~

When Berkshire acquired Central States Indemnity Co. of Omaha in 1992, William M. Kizer, Sr. described the negotiations this way: "The price he quoted us was that he buys companies for 10 times (annual) earnings. I suggested, 'Well, last year we made $10 million, so if my multiplication is right, that's $100 million,' and I gulped. And he said 'Okay.' And I said '$125 million?' He said, 'You're too late.'"[290]

SEEK INTRINSIC VALUE

Intrinsic value is a critical and at the same time an elusive concept:

> *"There is no formula to figure (intrinsic value) out. You have to know the business (whose stock you are considering buying)."[291]*

~

> *"Valuing a business is part art and part science."[292]*

~

> *"It doesn't have to be rock bottom to buy it. It has to be selling for less than you think the value of the business is, and it has to be run by honest and able people. But if you can buy into a business for less than it's worth today, and you're confident of the management, and you buy into a group of businesses like that, you're going to make money."[293]*

~

Don't worry about value investors snapping up all the bargains:

> *"I have seen no trend toward value investing in the 35 years I've practiced it. There seems to be some perverse human characteristic that likes to make easy things difficult."[294]*

~

EXPECT TO BE OUT OF STEP

"Berkshire buys when the lemmings are heading the other way."[295]

~

"Most people get interested in stocks when everyone else is. The time to get interested is when no one else is. You can't buy what is popular and do well."[296]

~

"You don't need to be a rocket scientist. Investing is not a game where the guy with the 160 IQ beats the guy with a 130 IQ. Rationality is essential."[297]

~

"Happily, there's more than one way to get to financial heaven."[298]

~ ✳ ~

THE USED-CIGAR-BUTT SCHOOL OF INVESTING

A Gentle Discourse between Walter Schloss and Warren Buffett:

A zealous student of Ben Graham at Columbia, Warren Buffett went to New Jersey for an annual meeting of a company in which Graham owned shares. Walter Schloss, who worked at Graham-Newman Co. also was there. They struck up a conversation, went to lunch, and have been friends ever since. Schloss later

101

left the Graham firm and went into business for himself. Buffett spotlighted Schloss's remarkable investment record in his now famous essay, "The Super Investors of Graham and Doddsville."

Through 39 years, thick and thin, Schloss has delivered a compound annual gain of just over 20 percent, compared to a Standard & Poors Industrials advance of just under 10 percent. Schloss keeps fund expenses at a minimum and forgoes management fees in years his funds make no gains. "I don't think I should get paid if I do a lousy job," Schloss says.[299]

"I think Walter's operational style should be a lesson for us all (one Charlie has already mastered). In effect, Walter is running an office for a year on what it costs Berkshire to start the engines on The Indefensible," Buffett said. [300]

The following is a condensed version of affectionate bantering between Buffett and Schloss at Benjamin Graham's 100th birthday memorial at the New York Society of Security Analysts. Buffett explained that Graham felt it was sort of cheating to use any tool, such as meetings with top management, that are not available to individual investors.

Buffett: I was inclined to cheat, but Walter has been more of a purist on that. Over the years, he's got some investment record, I'll tell you that!

Schloss: I really don't like talking to management. Stocks really are easier to deal with. They don't argue with you. They don't have emotional problems. You don't have to hold their hand. Now Warren is an unusual guy because he's not only a good analyst, he's a good salesman, and he's a very good judge of people. That's an unusual combination. If I were to (acquire) somebody with a business, I'm sure he would quit the very next day. I would misjudge his character or something—or I wouldn't understand that he really didn't like the business and really wanted to sell it and get out. Warren's people knock themselves out after he buys the business, so that's an unusual trait.

Schloss (later in the discussion): I own a lot of stocks. Warren doesn't *like* that, but I can't *help* it. You have to do what's comfortable for you, even if it's not as profitable as what Warren does. There's only one Warren. (Because Schloss owns so many stocks) the risk of any one is not that great. I try to buy securities that are undervalued based on assets more than earnings. I do a better job on assets than earnings because earnings have a way of changing.

Buffett (later in the conversation, not ready to give up on this): Walter has owned hundreds and hundreds and hundreds of securities. I call it the used-cigar-butt approach. You find these well-smoked, down-to-the-nub cigars, but they're free. You pick them up and get one free puff out of them. Anything is a buy at a price. Lately, Walter says that he has to buy an occasional new cigar. But he gets it on sale.[301]

Schloss on another occasion said of Buffett: "There's never been anything like him . . . the continued growth will be very hard. Maybe he'll merge it (Berkshire) with Canada."[302]

EARNINGS, EARNINGS, EARNINGS

Earnings, or a promise of future earnings, give stocks their value:

"We like stocks that generate high returns on invested capital where there is a strong likelihood that it will continue to do so. For example, the last time we bought Coca-Cola, it was selling at about 23 times earnings. Using our purchase price and today's earnings, that makes it about 5 times earnings. It's really the interaction of capital employed, the return on that capital, and future capital generated versus the purchase price today."[303]

～

"If the business does well, the stock eventually follows."[304]

～

Buffett explains that buying the stock of companies with strong earnings is a hedge against inflation:

"An irony of inflation-induced financial requirements is that the highly profitable companies—generally the best credits—require relatively little debt capital. But the laggards in profitability never can get enough. Lenders understand this problem much better than they did a decade ago—and are correspondingly less willing to let capital-hungry, low-profitability enterprises leverage themselves to the sky."[305]

～

One fiscal quarter does not an earnings trend make, as Buffett noted while discussing the direction of Salomon Inc.'s business:

"As long as we can make an annual 15 percent return on equity, I don't worry about one quarter's results."[306]

LOOK FORWARD, NOT BACK

"Pension fund managers continue to make investment decisions with their eyes firmly fixed on the rear-view mirror. This general fight-the-last-war approach has proven costly in the past and will likely prove equally costly this time around."[307]

~

"Of course, the investor of today does not profit from yesterday's growth."[308]

AVOID RISK

"I put heavy weight on certainty . . . if you do that, the whole idea of a risk factor doesn't make any sense to me. You don't do it where you take a significant risk. But it's not risky to buy securities at a fraction of what they're worth."[309]

~

Buffett often uses *The Washington Post* as an example of a risk-free investment. In 1973, the market price for the *Post* was $80 million and the company had no debt: "If you asked anyone in the business what (the *Post's*) properties were worth, they'd have said $400 million or something like that. You could have an auction in the middle of the Atlantic Ocean at 2:00 in the morning and you would have had people show up and bid that much for them. And it was being run by honest and able people who all had a significant part of their net worth in the business. It was ungodly safe. It wouldn't have bothered me to put my whole net worth in it. Not in the least."

"Risk comes from not knowing what you are doing."[310]

DON'T GAMBLE

"The propensity to gamble is always increased by a large prize versus a small entry fee, no matter how poor the true odds may be. That's why Las Vegas casinos advertise big jackpots and why state lotteries headline big prizes."[311]

∿

Some of the futures markets' products are nothing more than gambling games with a big skim for the casino owners: "And the more the activity, the greater the cost to the public and the greater the amount of money that will be left behind by them to be spread among the brokerage industry."[312]

∿

If you are drawn to the casino, watch what you drink:

"You're dealing with a lot of silly people in the marketplace; it's like a great big casino, and everyone else is boozing. If you can stick with Pepsi (these days he might say Coca-Cola), you should be okay."[313]

∿

Marshall Weinberg of the brokerage firm of Gruntal & Co. tells about going to lunch with Buffett in Manhattan: "He had an exceptional ham-and-cheese sandwich. A few days later, we were going out again. He said, 'Let's go back to that restaurant.' I said, 'But we were just there.' He said, 'Precisely. Why take a risk with another place? We know exactly what we're going to get.'" "That," says Weinberg, "is what Warren looks for in stocks too. He only invests in companies where the odds are great that they will not disappoint."[314]

∽

"People would rather be promised a (presumably) winning lottery ticket next week than an opportunity to get rich slowly."[315]

∽

Gambling in the market is treacherous for investors, and it has a negative effect on the national economy:

"We do not need more people gambling on the nonessential instruments identified with the stock market in the country, nor brokers who encourage them to do so. What we need are investors and advisers who look at the long-term prospects for an enterprise and invest accordingly. We need the intelligent commitment of investment capital, not leveraged market wagers. The propensity to operate in the intelligent, prosocial sectors of capital markets is deterred, not enhanced, by an active and exciting casino operating in somewhat the same arena, utiliz-

ing somewhat similar language, and serviced by the same workforce."[316]

WATCH FOR UNUSUAL CIRCUMSTANCES

"Great investment opportunities come around when excellent companies are surrounded by unusual circumstances that cause the stock to be misappraised."[317]

DON'T BE SURPRISED BY CIRCUMSTANCES

"It's only when the tide goes out that you learn who's been swimming naked."[318]

AVOID EXCESSIVE DEBT

Buffett calls borrowed money a dagger tied to a company's steering wheel pointed straight at its heart:

"You will someday hit a pothole."[319]

∼

Charlie Munger also has an opinion on debt: "Warren and I are chicken about buying stocks on margin. There's always a slight chance of catastrophe when you own securities pledged to others. The ideal is to borrow in a way no temporary thing can disturb you."[320]

∼

Buffett also says the U.S. trade deficit is a dangerously accruing debt that is secured by U.S. assets:

> *"Our riches are our curse in our attempts to attain a trade balance. If we were less well-off, commercial realities would constrain our trade deficit. Because we are rich, however, we can continue to trade earning properties for consumable trinkets. We are much like a wealthy farm family that annually sells acreage so that it can sustain a lifestyle unwarranted by its current output. Until the plantation is gone, it's all pleasure and no pain. In the end, however, the family will have traded the life of an owner for the life of a tenant farmer."[321]*

Buffett suggests a solution to the trade problem: a system of issuing import certificates when a certain value of goods is exported, whereby it would be necessary to have a certificate to import that same value of goods into the United States. The exporter could sell or trade his or her certificates to an importer. A buy-sell-or-barter system for the certificates would evolve, and imports and exports would always be of equal value. Buffett put forth his scheme in an op-ed piece in *The Washington Post* in 1987. Perhaps because the proposal would increase import prices and reduce U.S. consumption of foreign goods (getting a grip on our national impulse to consume more than we produce), there was no stampede to adopt Buffett's plan.

LOOK FOR SCREAMING BARGAINS

Authors who have written about Buffett's investment style tell how he measures the stream of cash that the company generates today and into the future, then, using a reasonable interest rate, discounts the cash flow back to the present. Is it possible that Buffett just clicks the calculations off in his head? Maybe. There seems to be no paper trail:

"Warren talks about these discounted cash flows ... I've never seen him do one," Munger huffed.

"It's true," replied Buffett. "If (the value of a company) doesn't just scream out at you, it's too close."[322]

ARBITRAGE WHEN POSSIBLE

"Because my mother isn't here tonight, I'll even confess to you that I have been an arbitrageur," Buffett said at a business seminar.[323] Buffett learned arbitrage during his early days at Graham-Newman. In its pure form, arbitrage is buying at a low price in one market and selling at a higher price in another. Buffett uses arbitrage when one company announces the acquisition of another company at a price higher than the current market quote:

"We look at the arbitrage deal, once something is announced. We look at what they've announced, what we think it will be worth, what we will have to pay, how long we're going to be in. We try to calculate the probability it will go through. That is the calculation: the name (of the companies involved) doesn't make much difference."[324]

BE PATIENT

"In investments, there's no such thing as a called strike. You can stand there at the plate and the pitcher can throw a ball right down the middle, and if it's General Motors at 47 and you don't know enough to decide on General Motors at 47, you let it go right on by and no one's going to call a strike. The only way you can have a strike is to swing and miss."[325]

~

"I've never swung at a ball while it's still in the pitcher's glove," Buffett said on another occasion.[326]

~

"You do things when the opportunities come along. I've had periods in my life when I've had a bundle of ideas come along, and I've had long dry spells. If I get an idea next week, I'll do something. If not, I won't do a damn thing."[327]

~

"You could be somewhere where the mail was delayed three weeks and do just fine investing."[328]

THINK FOR YOURSELF

Munger says that coming from Omaha, Buffett absorbed the attitude of a self-reliant pioneer: "Buffett believes successful investment is intrinsically independent in nature."[329]

~

How much attention does Buffett pay to the recommendation of brokers?

"Never ask the barber if you need a haircut."[330]

⌣

As for stock market forecasters:

"Forecasts usually tell us more of the forecaster than of the future."[331]

⌣

A constant stream of people ask Buffett to invest in their ideas. He replies:

"With my idea and your money, we'll do okay."[332]

⌣

When asked why he bought $139 million of Washington Public Power Supply System (WPPSS, also known as WHOOPS) junk bonds in 1983 and 1984 when ratings indicated they were a high risk:

"We don't make judgments based on ratings. If we wanted Moody's and Standard & Poor's to run our money, we'd give it to them."[333]

NOTE: The bonds, which did not default, offered a fixed 16.3 percent tax-free yield, resulting in a $22.7 million annual return.

⌣

Buffett and Munger make a committee of two, and at times even Charlie seems extraneous:

"My idea of a group decision is to look in the mirror."[334]

~

"If Fed Chairman Alan Greenspan were to whisper to me what his monetary policy was going to be over the next two years, it wouldn't change one thing I do."[335]

~

Especially don't listen to a computer:

"The more instruments that are designed, the smarter the players have to be."[336]

~

"You have to think for yourself. It always amazes me how high-IQ people mindlessly imitate. I never get good ideas talking to other people."[337]

~

If thinking for yourself becomes too difficult, Buffett borrows a suggestion from Goethe:

"When ideas fail, words come in very handy."[338]

HAVE THE RIGHT TOOLS

Buffett's suggestion to the independent investor is:

"You should have a knowledge of how business operates and the language of business (accounting),

113

some enthusiasm for the subject, and qualities of temperament which may be more important than IQ points. These will enable you to think independently and to avoid various forms of mass hysteria that infect the investment markets from time to time."[339]

~

Understanding the fundamentals of accounting is a form of self-defense:

"When managers want to get across the facts of the business to you, it can be done within the rules of accounting. Unfortunately, when they want to play games, at least in some industries, it can also be done within the rules of accounting. If you can't recognize the differences, you shouldn't be in the equity-picking business."[340]

BE WARY OF WALL STREET

"Wall Street is the only place that people ride to in a Rolls Royce to get advice from those who take the subway."[341]

~

"Full-time professionals in other fields, let's say dentists, bring a lot to the layman. But in aggregate, people get nothing for their money from professional money managers."[342]

~

"Wall Street likes to characterize the proliferation of frenzied financial games as a sophisticated, prosocial activity, facilitating the fine-tuning of a complex economy. But the truth is otherwise: Short-term transactions frequently act as an invisible foot, kicking society in the shins."[343]

Options traders are a favorite Buffett target:

"It has always been a fantasy of mine that a boatload of 25 brokers would be shipwrecked and struggle to an island from which there could be no rescue. Faced with developing an economy that would maximize their consumption and pleasure, would they, I wonder, assign 20 of their number to produce food, clothing, shelter, etc., while setting five to trading options endlessly on the future output of the 20?"[344]

"To many on Wall Street, both companies and stocks are seen only as raw materials for trades."[345]

Charlie Munger says he agrees with John Maynard Keynes, who called investment management a "low calling."

"Warren and I are a little different in that we actually run businesses and allocate capital to them. Keynes atoned for his 'sins' by making money for his college and serving his nation. I do my outside activities to atone, and Warren uses his investment success to be a great teacher. And we love to make money for the people who trusted us early on, when we were young and poor."[346]

ONLY BUY SECURITIES
THAT YOU UNDERSTAND

"Investment must be rational; if you can't understand it, don't do it."[347]

~

Asked about the use of derivatives as an investment vehicle, Buffett said that the danger is twofold: derivatives are seldom well understood by investors and they tend to involve heavy leverage:

"When you combine ignorance and borrowed money, the consequences can get interesting."[348]

~

"I want to be able to explain my mistakes. This means I do only the things I completely understand."[349]

~

Berkshire owned four million shares of General Foods Corporation, and in October 1985, captured profits of $332 million when the company was sold to Philip Morris Co. General Foods owns familiar brand names like Tang, Jell-O and Kool-Aid:

"I can understand Kool-Aid," Buffett said.

INVEST IN MARKETS
YOU CAN FATHOM

What goes for individual stocks also goes for stock markets. Though Buffett says he will look anywhere to find a good business, he usually shops domestically:

"We love the kinds of companies that can do well in international markets, obviously, particularly where they're largely untapped. Would we buy Coca-Cola if instead of being domiciled in Atlanta it was domiciled in London or Amsterdam or someplace? The answer of course is yes. Would I like it quite as well? The answer is just a tiny notch less. Because there might be nuances of corporate governance factors or tax factors or attitudes toward capitalists or anything else that I might not understand quite as well, even in England, as I might in the United States."[350]

∽

"It's hard enough to understand the peculiarities and complexities of the culture in which you've been raised, much less a variety of others. Anyway, most of our shareholders have to pay their bills in U.S. dollars."[351]

∽

Additionally, the U.S. equity market is huge:

"If I can't make money in a $5 trillion market, it may be a little bit of wishful thinking to think that

117

all I have to do is get a few thousand miles away and I'll start showing my stuff."[352]

BUILD A CIRCLE OF COMPETENCE

Here's how:

"Draw a circle around the businesses you understand and then eliminate those that fail to qualify on the basis of value, good management, and limited exposure to hard times."[353]

~

Next:

"I would take one industry at a time and develop some expertise in half a dozen. I would not take the conventional wisdom now about any industries as meaning a damn thing. I would try to think it through.

"If I were looking at an insurance company or a paper company, I would put myself in the frame of mind that I had just inherited that company, and it was the only asset my family was ever going to own.

"What would I do with it? What am I thinking about? What am I worried about? Who are my competitors? Who are my customers? Go out and talk to them. Find out the strengths and weaknesses of this particular company versus other ones.

"If you've done that, you may understand the business better than the management."[354]

~

118

"Our principles are valid when applied to technology stocks, but we don't know how to do it. If we are going to lose your money, we want to be able to get up here next year and explain how we did it. I'm sure Bill Gates would apply the same principles. He understands technology the way I understand Coca-Cola or Gillette. I'm sure he looks for a margin of safety. I'm sure he would approach it like he was owning a business and not just a stock. So our principles can work for any technology. We just aren't the ones to do it. If we can't find things within our circle of competence, we won't expand the circle. We'll wait."[355]

~

"Anybody who tells you they can value, you know, all the stocks in Value Line, and on the board, must have a very inflated idea of their own ability because it's not that easy. But if you spend your time focusing on some industries, you'll learn a lot about valuation."[356]

~

Staying within his circle of competence means that Buffett will miss certain good investments simply because he didn't have the skill or knowledge to evaluate the companies involved:

"I missed the play in cellular because cellular is outside of my circle of competence."[357]

~

"The most important thing in terms of your circle of competence is not how large the area of it is, but how well you've defined the perimeter. If you know where the edges are, you're way better off than somebody that's got one that's five times as large but they get very fuzzy about the edges."[358]

〜

A circle of competence can serve over a lifetime. In 1995, Berkshire acquired the 49 percent of GEICO it didn't already own. Buffett became interested in GEICO when he discovered that his professor, Ben Graham, was its chairman:

"When I was 20, I invested well over half of my net worth in GEICO."[359]

〜

When asked why he invested in insurance, a notoriously roller-coaster business: "Sometimes it's a good business—and that's not very often—and sometimes it's a terrible business."

It depends on how the risk is managed:

"I can go into an emergency ward and write life insurance if you let me charge enough of a premium."[360]

NOTE: Buffett is known for his skill at investing insurance float, the money that has been collected in premiums but not yet paid out in claims.

〜

BUY READING GLASSES

How does Buffett determine the value of a business:

"Do a lot of reading."[361]

∿

"I read annual reports of the company I'm looking at and I read the annual reports of the competitors— that is the main source of material."[362]

∿

When he first took an interest in GEICO, this is what Buffett did: "I read a lot. I was over at the library . . . I started with Bests' (insurance rating service) looking at a lot of companies, reading some books about it, reading annual reports, talking to (insurance specialists), talking to managements when I could."[363]

∿

Don't blame yourself, Buffett says, if you don't understand everything:

"It's not impossible to write (an accounting) footnote explaining deferred acquisition costs in life insurance or whatever you want to do. You can write it so you can understand it. If it's written so you can't understand it, I'm very suspicious. I won't invest in a company if I can't understand the footnote, because I know they don't want me to understand it."[364]

∿

BECOME AN INVESTIGATIVE REPORTER

Washington Post reporter Bob Woodward (of Watergate fame) once asked Buffett how he analyzed stocks:

> *"Investing is reporting. I told him to imagine he had been assigned an in-depth article about his own paper. He'd ask a lot of questions and dig up a lot of facts. He'd* know The Washington Post. *And that's all there is to it."*[365]

~

Buffett's research takes curious turns. He once sat behind the cash register at Ross's, his favorite Omaha steakhouse, counting how many customers used American Express cards.[366] Sometimes the research doesn't even seem like research:

> *"I remember I went to see* Mary Poppins *at a theater on Broadway at 45th at about 2:00 in the afternoon. I had a little attache case and everything. I got up to this woman at the ticket booth and said, 'I've got a kid around here someplace.' I was going to see if this (movie) could be run over and over again in the future."*[367]

KEEP IT SIMPLE

When a friend suggested Buffett try his hand at real estate, he replied:

"Why should I buy real estate when the stock market is so easy?"[368]

⁓

"(Value Investing) ideas seem so simple and commonplace. It seems like a waste to go to school and get a PhD in economics. It's a little like spending eight years in divinity school and having someone tell you the ten commandments are all that matter."[369]

⁓

When asked how he and Munger perform "due diligence" on companies they buy, Buffett said:

"If you have to go through too much investigation, something is wrong."

⁓

Charlie said they were once subpoenaed for their staff papers on an acquisition: "There weren't any papers. There wasn't any staff," Munger said.[370]

⁓

In 1986, Berkshire Hathaway ran a newspaper advertisement seeking companies to buy. It read:

"We use no staff, and we don't need to discuss your company with consultants, investment bankers, commercial bankers, etc. You will deal only with Charles Munger, vice chairman of Berkshire, and with me."[371]

~

"All there is to investing is picking good stocks at good times and staying with them as long as they remain good companies."[372]

~

"You don't need a rocket scientist. Investing is not a game where the guy with the 160 IQ beats the guy with 130 IQ."[373]

~

"Talking at business schools, I always say (students) would be better off if, when they got out of school, they got a ticket with 20 punches on it. And every time they make an investment decision it uses up a punch. You'll never use up all 20 punches if you save them for the great ideas."[374]

NOTE: *Forbes* columnist Mark Hulbert ran some numbers and determined that if you remove Buffett's 15 best decisions from the hundreds of others, his long-term performance would be mediocre.[375]

~

Charlie Munger says this about the simplicity theory: "If you believe what Warren says, you could teach the whole (portfolio management) course in a couple of weeks."[376]

~

THINK BIG

At the beginning of a Berkshire Hathaway annual meeting several years ago, Buffett tapped the microphone to see if it was on. "Testing . . . one million . . . two million . . . three million."[377]

～

"I made a study back when I ran an investment partnership of all our larger investments versus the smaller investments. The larger investments always did better than the smaller investments. There is a threshold of examination and criticism and knowledge that has to be overcome or reached in making a big decision that you can get sloppy about on small decisions. Somebody says 'I bought a hundred shares of this or that because I heard about it at a party the other night.' Well there is that tendency with small decisions to think you can do it for not very good reasons."[378]

～

"I can't be involved in 50 or 75 things. That's a Noah's Ark way of investing—you end up with a zoo that way. I like to put meaningful amounts of money in a few things."[379]

～

When describing the types of companies Berkshire likes to buy:

"We're looking for 747s, not model airplanes."[380]

"I'm like a basketball coach," Buffett explained. "I go out on the street and look for seven-footers. If some guy comes up to me and says, 'I'm five-six, but you ought to see me handle the ball,' I'm not interested."[381]

Large or small, the company must perform:

"I'd rather have a $10 million business making 15 percent than a $100 million business making 5 percent."[382]

KNOW WHAT YOU'RE LOOKING FOR

The Berkshire Hathaway advertisement for possible acquisitions that ran in *The Wall Street Journal* constituted a virtual checklist for value investors:

"Here's what we are looking for," the ad read:

1. Large purchases (at least $10 million of after-tax earnings, and preferably much more).

   NOTE: Individual investors can ignore the first one. It is there because small purchases can't make a blip on Berkshire's bottom line. The fact that individual investors can profit from smaller investments is an advantage, since it gives a much wider range of stocks from which to choose.

2. Demonstrated consistent earning power (future projections are of little interest to us, nor are "turnaround" situations).

3. Businesses earning good returns on equity while employing little or no debt.

4. Management in place (we can't supply it).

   NOTE: A subtle way of saying *good* management in place.

5. Simple businesses (if there's a lot of technology, we won't understand it).

6. An offering price (we don't want to waste our time or that of the seller by talking, even preliminarily, about a transaction when price is unknown).[383]

   NOTE: Luckily for small investors, Mr. Market shows up every workday with an offering price.

~

Each year in Berkshire Hathaway's annual report, Buffett publishes a similar list of traits of a business that would interest him. Occasionally the list is cast aside. It is, he says, ". . . a lot like selecting a wife. You can thoughtfully establish certain qualities you'd like her to have, then all of a sudden, you meet someone and you do it."[384]

DON'T SWEAT THE MATH

Buffett says that because he never studied calculus he's forced to agree with those who say that higher math skill is not needed for successful investing:

127

"If calculus were required, I'd have to go back to delivering papers. I've never seen any need for algebra. Essentially, you're trying to figure out the value of a business. It's true that you have to divide by the number of shares outstanding, so division is required. If you were going out to buy a farm or an apartment house or a dry cleaning establishment, I really don't think you'd have to take someone along to do calculus. Whether you made the right purchase or not would depend on the future earning ability of that enterprise, and then relating that to the price you are being asked for the asset."[385]

~

"Read Ben Graham and Phil Fisher, read annual reports, but don't do equations with Greek letters in them."[386]

~

If higher math is unimportant in selecting stocks, why are academic and professional journals dense with quantitative analysis? Buffett replied:

"Every priesthood does it. How could you be on top if no one is on the bottom?"[387]

~

Buffett's mathless philosophy did not come naturally. He developed it after he'd tried everything else:

"I used to chart all kinds of stocks, the more numbers the better."[388]

⁓

As a teenager Buffett was fascinated by technical information. This interest led to the publication of Buffett's first article. He was 17:

"There was an item (in Barron's) saying that if we would send along a description of how we used their statistical material they would publish some of them and pay $5. I wrote up something about how I used odd-lot figures. That $5 was the only money I ever made using statistics."[389]

ADMIRE FRUGALITY

"Whenever I read about some company undertaking a cost-cutting program, I know it's not a company that really knows what costs are all about. Spurts don't work in this area. The really good manager does not wake up in the morning and say, 'This is the day I'm going to cut costs,' any more than he wakes up and decides to practice breathing."[390]

⁓

Berkshire Hathaway owns about 7 percent of the stock of San Francisco-based Wells Fargo. News reached Munger that Wells Fargo CEO Carl Reichardt discovered one of his executives wanted to buy a Christmas tree for the office. Reichardt told him to buy it with his own money.

"When we heard that," said Munger, "we bought more stock."[391]

~

For Buffett, frugality begins at home. At the 1996 Berkshire annual meeting, he observed:

"Your board has collectively lost 100 pounds in the last year. They must have been trying to live on their director's fees."[392]

~

Buffett wrote the introduction to Alan C. (Ace) Green-berg's book, *Memos from the Chairman* in which a fictional character, Haimchinkel Malintz Anaynikal, goaded Bear Stearns employees not to waste resources:

"Haimchinkel is my kind of guy—cheap, smart, opinionated. I just wish I'd met him earlier in life, when, in the foolishness of my youth, I used to discard paper clips. But it's never too late, and I now slavishly follow and preach his principles," wrote Buffett.[393]

~

The quest for quality and the need for frugality need not cancel each other out, as Buffett noted when talking about programming at ABC:

"The funny thing is, better shows don't cost that much more than lousy shows."[394]

~

Sports shows also could be aired for less money:

"My guess is that the quality of football would be identical if we'd been paying 20 percent less for the football rights. It's just that all the football players would be earning a little less money. Ty Cobb played for $20,000 a year. In the end, if there's 20 percent less money available for sports programming, it will largely come out of the players."[395]

~

Buffett also applies thriftiness to his own financial affairs. He and Capital Cities/ABC chairman Thomas Murphy had walk-on parts for the ABC television soap opera, *All My Children*, with soap queen Susan Lucci in 1993. They were each paid about $300 for their performances:

When handed his check Murphy said, "I'm going to frame this." Buffett said, "I'm going to frame the stub."[396]

SET REALISTIC GOALS

Buffett says a growth rate of 15 percent per year is realistic, though not always easy for him to achieve:

"If we are to have a 15 percent gain, we have to make $400 million (a year) before tax, or $300 mil-

lion net, which is about a million a day—and I'm spending today here."[397]

NOTE: In fact, he usually does achieve it; in some years, Buffett nearly doubles his goal.

FACE FACTS

Don't take the performance of your stock personally. After all:

"A stock doesn't know you own it."[398]

~

Buffett has good reason for his interest in entertainment and leisure-oriented businesses:

"The market will pay you better to entertain than to educate."

Case in point: Berkshire's World Book encyclopedia has difficulty delivering the same stellar returns that the Disney Company achieves.[399]

~

When Buffett is asked at Berkshire annual meetings why he doesn't split the company's high-priced shares, people murmur to one another, "Here comes the pizza story."

The question, Buffett says, reminds him of a diner who asks the pizza maker to cut his pie into four slices rather than eight, since he "couldn't possibly eat eight."[400]

HE TELLS THEM BUT THEY DON'T LISTEN

Every year in Berkshire Hathaway's annual report, and again at the shareholder's meeting, Buffett warns investors not to expect too much of Berkshire's performance:

1985: "I can guarantee we will not do as well as in the past," Buffett told shareholders at the annual meeting. "I still think we may be able to do better than American industry as a whole."[401]

In the preceding year, Berkshire's gain was a weak 13.6 percent, compared to a 22 percent average annual increase in the previous 20 years. In 1986, Berkshire chalked up a 48.2 percent gain.

1992: Charlie Munger told *Business Week:* "Size at a certain point gets to be an anchor, which drags you down. We always knew that it would."[402] Berkshire's share price rose 20.3 percent in 1992.

1995: At Berkshire Hathaway's annual meeting, Buffett cautioned: "The future performance of Berkshire Hathaway won't come close to matching the performance of the past." He explained that "a fat wallet, however, is the enemy of superior results." And anyhow, "We don't have to keep getting rich at the same rate."[403]

1996: Berkshire's shares traded as high as $38,000. By mid-1996, the shares had retreated to $32,000.

EXPECT CHANGE

"Anything that can't go on forever will end."[404]

~

When he first started as a professional investor, Buffett says small-size investments made sense and he found a lot of stocks to buy. The economies of scale have now changed:

"I was overstimulated in the early days. I'm understimulated now."[405]

~

When asked what he thought of the wave of U.S. corporate downsizing, Buffett noted that American industry has always tried to do more with less. Change is unavoidable, but:

"It's no fun being a horse when the tractor comes along, or the blacksmith when the car comes along."

Turn the question backward, says Charlie Munger: "Name a business that has been ruined by downsizing. I can't name one. Name a company that has been ruined by bloat. I can name dozens."[406]

~

Buffett agrees that it is sometimes wise to look at problems from the opposite direction:

"It's like singing country western songs backward. That way you get your home back, your auto back, your wife back, and so forth . . ."[407]

Nevertheless, Buffett and Munger like industries in which change is limited, or at least manageable: "Take chewing gum for example," Buffett says. "Folks chew the same way today that they did 20 years ago. Nobody's come up with a new technique for that."[408]

BE CAPABLE OF CHANGE

When asked why he abandoned some value investing principles, Buffett replied:

> *"As we work with larger sums of money, it simply is not possible to stay with those subworking capital types of situations. It requires learning more about what's going to produce steady and increasing flows of cash in the future—if you are working with small sums of money, you don't even have to work that hard. We (at Graham-Newman) used to have a one-page sheet where you put down all the numbers on a company, and if it met certain tests of book value, working capital, and earnings, you bought it. It was that simple."[409]*

Buffett did not abruptly abandon the teachings of Graham and his co-author David Dodd:

> *"I evolved. I didn't go from ape to human or human to ape in a nice even manner."[410]*

~ ✳ ~

BABY BERKSHIRE SHARES

During the 1990s, Berkshire Hathaway's share price rode on the wings of a soaring market, finally peaking at just over $38,000 in March 1996 (shares traded for $8,550 in mid-1989). Despite the dizzying climb, Warren Buffett stood firm on his refusal to split shares, a step that would make it easier for new investors to buy and existing investors to sell. He said he didn't want Berkshire in the hands of speculators, and the most effective deterrent he could think of was a steep share price. Buffett signed birthday cards with the line, "May you live until Berkshire shares split."

Buffett held true to his word, but within a few weeks of the 1996 price peak, outside events compelled him to create the moral equivalent of a split. That spring Buffett announced he would issue B shares or secondary common shares of Berkshire Hathaway stock. The new shares were issued at one-thirtieth the price of the existing, or A shares. The only features that make B shares secondary are the lack of voting rights and the fact that B shareholders are ineligible for Berkshire's charitable giving program. Voting rights are unimportant since Buffett and Munger have enough shares to outvote all other holders. And who in his or her right mind would vote against Buffett and Munger anyway?

The advantage to A shareholders is that they can convert to 30 B shares at any time, no matter what the prices of the two shares are. B shareholders, however, are not allowed to convert to A shares, even if holders own 30 of them.

Buffett expects that arbitrage action between the two types of shareholders will keep the A and B share prices in perpetual 1-to-30 balance.

What made Buffett modify his plans was a scheme by several investment firms to create unit trusts from a pool composed entirely of Berkshire shares. Investors would buy the bite-size portions of Berkshire for $1,000 per unit and pay annual fees, plus up-front commissions of as much as 5 percent. Investors could hold the units until a 10-year maturity date or trade them on the New York Stock Exchange like any other security. The unit trusts were to be marketed to small investors hoping to participate in the remarkable gains enjoyed by those who discovered Berkshire Hathaway early on.

Speculation is speculation, even if it is once removed, in Buffett's view. "We do not want people to come in and think it's a hot stock and it will be a lot higher in a year."[411]

Or, more specifically: "There are people who think it (Berkshire's phenomenal share price growth) can happen again from this kind of base, and it's mathematically impossible," Buffett said. "We don't want to appeal subliminally to people who harbor these hopes."[412]

Critics said Buffett's controlling nature caused his reaction. Others said he was just being consistent. Buffett always said he wanted dedicated shareholders. "It gets down to attracting the highest-grade shareholder we can get."[413]

In a letter of protest to Five Sigma Investment Partners of Bala Cynwyd, Pennsylvania, one of the firms that proposed such a unit trust, Charlie Munger wrote: "Your trust . . . would entice many small investors into an investment unsuitable for them and overwhelmingly likely to leave large numbers feeling disappointed and abused."

Munger added: "Berkshire's stock price is now risky because (of) dramatic appreciation . . . since 1992 at a rate far higher than any increase in the stock's intrinsic value . . . . If he were asked by a friend or family member whether he advised a new purchase of Berkshire shares at the current price, Mr. Buffett would answer, 'No.'"[414] Munger said he feared aggressive sales efforts would act like "gasoline poured on a fire." When it appeared that Five Sigma would not back off, war broke out. Buffett announced the B share offering. "Berkshire intends to provide a direct, low-cost means of investment in Berkshire so superior to the investments offered by the unit trust promoters that their products will be rendered unmarketable," the prospectus for the shares read.[415]

To discourage brokers from hyping the new stock, Berkshire arranged the offering through Salomon. The commission was purposely set low, giving little incentive to brokers to push investors into the initial public offering. Additionally, Buffett said the company would issue as many shares as the public wanted, thus minimizing the first-week price spike caused by a limited supply and a high demand.

On the front page of the prospectus, Buffett repeated Munger's message to Five Sigma: "Management does not believe that the company's stock is undervalued."[416]

At the 1996 annual meeting, a shareholder asked about Berkshires's shares being overvalued. Buffett replied that he had not said the shares were overvalued. He said they were "not undervalued." There's a distinction, Buffett insisted, obviously rankled that the subtlety had been missed by journalists and investors alike.

The distinction seemed fuzzy to many in the investment world. "There are a lot of questions legitimately as to why he's doing this," said Derek Sasveld, a consultant at Ibbotson Associates Inc., a Chicago stock research and consulting firm. "It doesn't seem to be a completely logical situation."[417]

William LeFevre, senior market analyst at Ehrenkrantz King Nussbaum Inc. in New York, suspected Buffett's territory had been invaded. "His credibility is as high as it gets, and he doesn't want somebody making a buck off the name of Warren Buffett."[418]

Others, however, saw the structure of the vehicle, rather than the intrinsic value of the stock, as the source of Buffett's problem. At the 1996 annual meeting, Buffett described the unit trusts as "a high commission product with substantial annual fees."

"Mr. Buffett has always been a champion of shareholder rights and he doesn't like the fact that to buy into the unit investment trusts is not as economically feasible as buying the common stock," said James Mulvey, an analyst at Dresdner Securities USA Inc.

With the Baby B's, as investors called them, the same deal could be had with only the payment of a broker's commission.

Barron's columnist Alan Abelson dismissed the "not undervalued" statement—plus prospectus disclaimers that the company's intrinsic value could continue to grow at past rates—as mere pandering to regulators. "To Warren Buffett we say, truth wounds, cynicism kills—think on what ye have wrought and repent! There's still time to revise that prospectus. A small phrase—'just kidding!'—inserted on the front page right below those caveats will do the trick."[419]

Others, however, thought Buffett might have been understating the overvaluation problem. Stock market columnist Malcolm Berko ran a brief analysis of Berkshire for his readers, describing it as a closed-end mutual fund. Berko estimated that Berkshire (both A and B) was selling at a massive premium over its net asset value (NAV). Berko estimated the NAV of Berkshire A shares at $15,000. "So, in my opinion, you gotta be dumber than a bag of ball-peen hammers to pay a $21,000 premium over NAV to own BRKA," Berko wrote.[420]

This debate over the value of Berkshire's share price had an impact on the stock. The A shares quickly receded from a high of $38,000 back to the $33,000 range. The B shares were issued at $1,110. There was a price hop shortly after the offering, but the shares settled in at just over $1,000 within a few weeks.

The Berkshire B stock sold like ice in Arizona despite Buffett's frank—though somewhat perplexing—disclosure as to the intrinsic value of Berkshire Hathaway. At first, the company said it would issue 100,000 shares, but that number was increased four times. Ultimately, more than 517,500 were issued, doubling Berkshire's shareholder base to 80,000 individuals. There is no word as to what Buffett will do with the approximately $600 million collected or on where the 1997 annual meeting will be held now that shareholder base has expanded. At the last meeting before the offering, shareholders split the seams of the Holiday Inn Convention Center, Omaha's largest hall.

ADMIT YOUR MISTAKES

Buffett confesses to dozens of investment errors, including buying Berkshire Hathaway, a New England textile mill. The lagging textile business was finally closed down, but the corporate structure and name was retained as an investment vehicle. Investor Irving Kahn, who has known Buffett since his student days, observed, "Even a man with Warren's talents slips."[421]

~

Buffett takes his lumps with good humor:

> *"Of course some of you probably wonder why we are now buying Capital Cities at $172.50 per share given that this author, in a characteristic burst of brilliance, sold Berkshire's holdings in the same company at $43 per share in 1978–80. Anticipating your question, I spent a lot of time working on a snappy answer that would reconcile these acts.*
>
> *"A little more time please."*[422]

~

> *"I've repressed my memory of the earlier sale of Cap Cities stock."*[423]

~

Buffett occasionally gives bum advice: "My only role with *The Washington Post's* sale of cellular phone properties was to recommend against the original purchase of the properties at one-fifth the price they sold for. And that's the last time they asked me. They didn't pay attention to me the first time and they didn't ask the second time."[424]

~

Buffett says his mistakes of omission are more bothersome than errors of commission: "The mistakes you don't see in our case are way bigger than the mistakes that you see. We owned 5 percent of the Walt Disney Company in 1966. The whole Disney Company was selling for $80 million in 1966, debt free: $4 million bought us 5 percent of the company. They spent $17 million on the Pirates (of the Caribbean) ride in 1966. Here was a company selling at less than five times rides, and they had lots of rides. I mean, *that* is cheap."[425]

NOTE: Buffett invested in Walt Disney in 1966 at a split-adjusted price of 31 cents per share. Thirty years later, when Berkshire Hathaway acquired 20 million shares in Disney in its merger with Cap Cities/ABC, the shares were trading at $65. Buffett sold his 31-cent shares at 48 cents.

"Oh, well. It's nice to be back," Buffett said.[426]

JOIN AA (AIRLINES ANONYMOUS)

In 1995, Buffett took a $268.5 million write-off for 75 percent of his $385 million investment in USAir. The shares' 9.25 percent dividend had not been paid since September 1994. In the spring of 1996, Buffett was searching for a buyer for the convertible preferred stock: "That was a senior security. It was a mistake, but it wasn't a common equity we picked as a wonderful business. There aren't that many wonderful businesses in the world."[427]

~

The USAir problem brought home another point to Buffett:

"Frankly, no airline is going to be a wonderful business."[428]

~

Buffett explained in a speech in North Carolina why airlines are not an investor's friend: "The interesting thing of course is that if you go back to the time—and we're in the right state for that—from Kitty Hawk, net, the airline transport business in the United States has made no money. Just think if you'd been down there at Kitty Hawk and you'd seen this guy go up, and all of a sudden this vision hits you that tens of millions of people would be doing this all over the world someday. It would bring us all closer together and everything. You'd think, my god, this is something to be in on. Despite putting in billions and billions and billions of dollars, the net return to owners for the entire airline industry, if you'd owned it all, and you'd put up all this money, is less than zero. If there had been a capitalist down there, the guy should have shot down Wilbur. One small step for mankind and one huge step back for capitalism."[429]

~

Buffett attributes his USAir purchase to temporary insanity. How will he fend off a future attack?

> *"So now I have this 800 number, and if I ever have the urge to buy an airline stock, I dial this number and I say my name is Warren and I'm an airoholic. Then this guy talks me down on the other end."*[430]

~

Marshall Lewis of the investment firm Blunt, Ellis & Loewi offered these words of comfort following the USAir write-down: "Buffett still walks on water. He just splashes a little bit."[431]

NOTE: In July 1996, USAir reported its best quarterly profit ever. The airline said it would again make a dividend payment to Berkshire Hathaway and other owners of preferred shares.

LEARN FROM YOUR MISTAKES

Buffett says he made one of his worst decisions at age 21 when he put 20 percent of his net worth in a gasoline station. Over the years, he figures, the error cost him about $800 million in lost economic opportunity.[432]

The first step to recovery is to stop doing the wrong thing:

> *"It's an old principle. You don't have to make it back the way you lost it."*[433]

~

Berkshire does not pay dividends to investors. They thus avoid double taxation, and with no effort on their part, continually reinvest their earnings. The exception was a 10-cent dividend Buffett paid to his partnership in 1967. Of that, he says: "I must have been in the bathroom at the time."[434]

NOTE: Buffett says that if the time comes when he believes shareholders can find more lucrative ways to invest than Berkshire can, he will pay a dividend.

∼

The Salomon government bond scandal taught Buffett a lesson that he might have preferred to skip:

"You won't believe this—because I don't look that dumb—but I volunteered for the job of interim chairman. It's not what I want to be doing, but it will be what I will be doing until it gets done properly."[435]

∼

A battalion of lawyers filing suits against Salomon helped focus Buffett's attention:

"I may be the American Bar Association's Man of the Year before the year is over."[436]

∼

Buffett compared the year he spent in New York helping Salomon Brothers get back on its feet to war: "You do it because you have to, but you're not looking for another one."[437]

∼

Before the Salomon incident occurred, Buffett was asked why he made biting remarks about the banking industry, when Berkshire held a big stake in Salomon, Buffett replied:

> *"Why are we vocal critics of the investment banking business when we have a $700 million investment in Salomon? I guess atonement is probably the answer."*[438]

BUY STORYBOOK STOCKS

Buffett's favorite way of describing intrinsic value and margin of safety implies that he has spent much time studying the Walt Disney Company, a storybook scenario if there ever was one. His favorite companies, Buffett says, are like:

> *"Wonderful castles, surrounded by deep, dangerous moats where the leader inside is an honest and decent person. Preferably, the castle gets its strength from the genius inside; the moat is permanent and acts as a powerful deterrent to those considering an attack; and inside, the leader makes gold but doesn't keep it all for himself. Roughly translated, we like great companies with dominant positions, whose franchise is hard to duplicate and has tremendous staying power or some permanence to it."*[439]

~

> *"You need a moat in business to protect you from the guy who is going to come along and offer it (your product) for a penny cheaper."*[440]

(For more on moats, see "Appreciate Franchise Value" and "Respect Pricing Power.")

~

Buffett performed a real-world analysis on his favorite storybook stock back in 1969:

> *"When I buy a stock, I think of it in terms of buying a whole company, just as if I were buying the store down the street. If I were buying the store, I'd want to know all about it. I mean, look at what Walt Disney was worth on the stock market in the first half of 1966. The price per share was $53 and this didn't look especially cheap, but on that basis you could buy the whole company for $80 million when* Snow White, Swiss Family Robinson, *and some other cartoons, which had been written off the books, were worth that much (by themselves); and then (in addition), you had Disneyland and Walt Disney, a genius, as a partner."*[441]

~

Following the 1996 merger of Cap Cities/ABC with Disney, Berkshire again held a strong position in Disney:

> *"Owning* Snow White *(the movie) is like owning an oil field. You pump it out and sell it and then it seeps back in again."*

NOTE: Disney finds it can re-issue *Snow White* every seven years.

And then there's Mickey Mouse:

"The nice thing about the mouse is that he doesn't have an agent. You own the mouse. He's yours."[442]

SEEK EXCELLENT COMPANIES

"You should invest in a business that even a fool can run, because someday a fool will."[443]

~

"In any business, there are going to be all kinds of factors that happen next week, next month, next year, and so forth. But the really important thing is to be in the right business. The classic case is Coca-Cola, which went public in 1919. They initially sold stock at $40 a share. The next year, it went down to $19. Sugar prices had changed pretty dramatically after World War I. So you would have lost half of your money one year later if you'd bought the stock when it first came public; but if you owned that share today—and had reinvested all of your dividends—it would be worth about $1.8 million. We have had depressions. We have had wars. Sugar prices have gone up and down. A million things have happened. How much more fruitful is it for us to think about whether the product is likely to sustain itself and its economics than to try to be questioning whether to jump in or out of the stock?"[444]

~

"Let's say you were going away for 10 years and you wanted to make one investment and you know everything you know now, and you couldn't change it while you're gone. What would you think about?

"I came up with anything in terms of certainty, where I knew the market was going to continue to grow, where I knew the leader was going to continue to be the leader—I mean worldwide—and where I knew there would be big unit growth, I just don't know anything like Coke."[445]

∼

"Charlie (Munger) made me focus on the merits of a great business with tremendously growing earning power, but only when you can be sure of it—not like Texas Instruments or Polaroid, where the earning power was hypothetical."[446]

∼

Buffett explained to General Foods President Philip Smith why he was buying the company's stock when nobody else was interested:

"You've got strong brand names, you're selling three times earnings when other food companies are selling at six to seven times earnings, and you're loaded with cash. If you don't know what to do with it, someone else will."[447]

∼

"The definition of a great company is one that will be great for 25 or 30 years."[448]

~

One reason for buying excellent companies (in addition to strong growth) is that once a purchase is made, the investor has only to sit back and trust the company's managers to do their jobs. In 1973, Buffett already owned a good-size chunk of Berkshire, plus a bank in Illinois, an Omaha weekly newspaper, interest in a half-dozen insurance companies, a trading stamp company, a chain of women's clothing stores, and a candy company. Yet he told a reporter, with no boastfulness:

"I can almost do it with my hands in my pockets. I really live a pretty easy life."[449]

~

"I tell everybody who works for our company to do only two things to be successful. They are 1) think like an owner, and 2) tell us bad news right away. There is no reason to worry about the good news."[450]

STICK WITH QUALITY

"It's far better to own a portion of the Hope diamond than 100 percent of a rhinestone."[451]

~

From his boyhood, when he published a tipsheet called "Stableboy Selections," Buffett has shown an interest in horse racing:

"There are speed handicappers and class handicappers. The speed handicapper says you try and figure out how fast the horse can run. A class handicapper says a $10,000 horse will beat a $6,000 horse. Graham says, 'buy any stock cheap enough and it will work.' That was the speed handicapper. And other people said, 'Buy the best company, and it will work.' That's class handicapping."[452]

NOTE: Buffett began as a speed handicapper but progressed to class handicapping.

∼

When asked what he thought of junk bonds:

"I think they'll live up to their name."[453]

APPRECIATE FRANCHISE VALUE

Buffett describes franchise value as a moat around the castle of business. He uses Gillette as an illustration:

"There are 20 to 21 billion razor blades used in the world a year. Thirty percent of those are Gillettes, but 60 percent by value are Gillettes. They have 90 percent market shares in some countries—in Scandinavia and Mexico. Now, when something has been around as

151

long as shaving and you find a company that has both that kind of innovation, in terms of developing better razors all the time, plus the distribution power, and the position in people's minds. . . . You know, here's something you do every day—I hope you do it every day—for $20 bucks (per year) you get a terrific shaving experience. Now men are not inclined to shift around when they get that kind of situation."[454]

~

"You go to bed feeling very comfortable just thinking about two and a half billion males with hair growing while you sleep. No one at Gillette has trouble sleeping."[455]

~

If you didn't grasp the concept of franchise value with Gillette, try it with Hershey bars:

"If (you go into a store and) they say 'I don't have Hershey bar, but I have this unmarked chocolate bar that the owner of the place recommends,' if you'll walk across the street to buy a Hershey bar or if you'll pay a nickel more for the (Hershey) bar than the unmarked bar or something like that, that's franchise value."[456]

~

Or try the sweetheart test. There are times when a bargain price isn't the point:

". . . you know this. They're not going to go home on Valentine's Day and say 'Here honey, here are two

pounds of chocolates. I took the low bid.' It just doesn't work. "[457]

~

Coca-Cola has the strongest franchise value of any company on the planet:

"If you run across one good idea for a business in your lifetime, you're lucky; and fundamentally, this (Coca-Cola) is the best large business in the world. It has got the most powerful brand in the world. It sells for an extremely moderate price. It's universally liked—the per capita consumption goes up almost every year in almost every country. There is no other product like it." [458]

~

"If you gave me $100 billion and said take away the soft drink leadership of Coca-Cola in the world, I'd give it back to you and say it can't be done." [459]

~

The moat of franchise power offers strong protection:

"A takeover (of Coca-Cola) would be like Pearl Harbor." [460]

~

At least twice Buffett has acquired an interest in companies that faced serious financial difficulties, a condition that did not alter their franchise value:

"It was similar to American Express in late 1963 when the salad oil scandal hit it. It did not hurt the franchise of the travelers check or the credit card. It could have ruined the balance sheet of American Express but the answer of course was that American Express with no net worth was worth a tremendous amount of money.

"And GEICO with no net worth was worth a tremendous amount of money, too, except it might get closed up the next day because it had no net worth, but I was satisfied that the net worth would be there. The truth is, a lot of insurance companies for the ownership of it would have put up the net worth. We would have put it up."[461]

NOTE: In 1976, GEICO hit rough water after growing so fast; the company outpaced its capabilities. It recovered after Buffett bought in.

$\sim$

Buffett has lost interest in certain franchises. He once was one of RJR Nabisco's (owners of Reynolds Tobacco) largest shareholders, but disposed of the shares in the early 1980s. Though he reportedly didn't object to Salomon Inc. making an RJR Nabisco investment in 1988, he declined to join. He is reported to have said:

"I'll tell you why I like the cigarette business. It costs a penny to make. Sell it for a dollar. It's addictive. And there's fantastic brand loyalty."[462]

NOTE: Buffett later said he was quoting another person as having said this, and meant the statement to be ironical.

RESPECT PRICING POWER

A good business, Buffett explains, enjoys price flexibility. Pricing power is a kissing cousin to franchise value:

> *"If you own See's Candy, and you look in the mirror and say, 'mirror, mirror on the wall, how much do I charge for candy this fall,' And it says 'more,' that's a good business."*[463]

~

In 1986, Buffett anticipated the problems that would soon beleaguer the television industry due to its weakness in pricing power:

> *"Essentially, TV had a lot of untapped pricing power many years ago, and they used it all up. They probably went a little beyond it. So the ability to price is not there to the same degree. I do not see galloping revenue gains beyond inflation in the network business; for years, they were getting it and they developed a way of life that was predicated upon it. And now you're seeing an adjustment."*[464]

FIND A COMPANY WITH CHEAP FLOAT (THEN TRY TO NOT MISPLACE THE COMPANY)

Buffett learned early that insurance company profits are based on superior investing of the premiums that accumulate awaiting the payment of a claim. This float, from all of Berkshire Hathaway's insurance businesses, is around $6.5 billion, and GEICO, which is now wholly owned by Berkshire, has produced $3 billion of it. The excess money does not belong to Berkshire Hathaway, but can be used by it.

"It has been a big mistake (by some securities analysts) to think of the value of the insurance operation as its book value alone, without regard to the value of the float," Buffett said.[465]

~

Float exists in other businesses as well. "Blue Chip Stamp used to be that kind of a business until it disappeared one day. Where was it? In the closet? I don't know," Buffett said.

NOTE: Trading stamps were popular as a grocery shopping incentive in the 1950s and 1960s, but lost ground to coupons and other gimmicks. However, before Blue Chip disappeared, Buffett had made considerable profit investing the float.[466]

LEARN TO LIKE MONOPOLY

Freddie Mac (the Federal Home Loan Mortgage Corp.), a quasipublic corporation, provides a secondary market for home mortgages. Freddie Mac and its sister agency, Fannie Mae (Federal National Mortgage Assn.) control 90 percent of this business. The industry is a duopoly:

"It's the next best thing to a monopoly."[467]

~

"Newspapers are a marvelous business. It's one of the few businesses that tend toward a natural, limited monopoly. Obviously, it competes with other advertising forms, but not with anything exactly like itself. Show me another business like that—there isn't one."

NOTE: Buffett made the preceding comment in 1986. Because of fundamental changes in demographics, retailing, and a proliferation of competing advertising possibilities, Buffett has bumped newspapers down into a "good but not great" category.

～

During a circulation war between *The Buffalo Evening News* and the competing *Courier-Express*, the latter sued, accusing Buffett's newspaper of price fixing. A sore point was the rumor that Buffett had said owning a monopoly newspaper was like owning an unregulated toll bridge. When the comment came up in court, Buffett said:

"I have said in an inflationary world that a toll bridge would be a great thing to own if it was unregulated."

Why, asked the opposing attorney.

"Because you have laid out the capital costs. You build the bridge in old dollars and you don't have to keep replacing it."[468]

～

FIND MANAGERS WHO THINK
LIKE OWNERS

"I always picture myself as owning the whole place. And if management is following the same policy that I would follow if I owned the whole place, that's a management I like."[469]

~

"The best CEOs love operating their companies and don't prefer going to Business Round Table meetings or playing golf at Augusta National."[470]

~

Buffett often says that because he's not an expert in candy sales, encyclopedia publishing, the uniform or shoe business (all of which Berkshire owns), he likes managers who are. Of H. H. Brown, shoe manufacturers and a major buyer of leather, Buffett says:

"When a single steer topples, they know it."[471]

MANAGEMENT IS IMPORTANT, BUT
A GOOD COMPANY IS MORE IMPORTANT

"Our conclusion is that, with few exceptions, when management with a reputation for brilliance tackles a business with a reputation for poor fundamental economics, it is the reputation of the business that remains intact."[472]

~

"*I like a business that, when it's not managed at all, still makes lots of money. That's my kind of business.*"[473]

AVOID THE INSTITUTIONAL IMPERATIVE (THE TENDENCY FOR CORPORATIONS TO ACT LIKE LEMMINGS)

"*Any business craving of the leader, however foolish, will be quickly supported by .... studies prepared by his troops.*"[474]

~

"*If you have mediocrity and you have a bunch of friends on the board, it's certainly not the kind of test you put a football team through. If the coach of a football team puts 11 lousy guys out on the field, he loses his job. The board never loses their job because they've got a mediocre CEO. So, you've got none of that self-cleansing type of operation that works with all the other jobs.*"[475]

FAVOR COMPANIES THAT REPURCHASE THEIR OWN STOCK

When a company's own shares are trading at less than intrinsic value, Buffett says one of the best investments the company can make is to buy back its own shares. Does this mean he will acquire Berkshire shares if the price falls below intrinsic value?

"That would make sense and I would do it, but

only if Berkshire is cheaper than other stocks I'm interested in at the time."[476]

DON'T WORRY ABOUT DIVERSIFICATION

"Diversification is a protection against ignorance. (It) makes very little sense for those who know what they're doing."[477]

~

"A lot of great fortunes in the world have been made by owning a single wonderful business. If you understand the business, you don't need to own very many of them."[478]

~

Buffett quotes Broadway impresario Billy Rose in explaining the difficulties of over-diversification: "If you have a harem of 40 women, you never get to know any of them very well."[479]

INVEST FOR THE LONG TERM

Buffett so deplores short-term trading that he has suggested a 100-percent tax on profits made on stock held for less than one year.[480]

~

"Charlie and I expect to hold our stock for a very long time. In fact, you may see us up here when (we're so old that) neither of us knows who the other guy is."[481]

"Now when you read about Boone Pickens and Jimmy Goldsmith and the crew, they talk about creating value for shareholders. They aren't creating value; they are transferring it from society to shareholders. That may be a good or bad thing but it isn't creating value—it's not like Henry Ford developing the car or Ray Kroc figuring out how to deliver hamburgers better than anyone else . . . . In the last few years . . . one (company) after another has been transformed by people who have understood this game. That means that every citizen owes a touch more of what is needed to pay for all the goods and services that the government provides."[490]

WHEN REWARDS ARE DISPROPORTIONATE

Other people make equally valuable contributions to the safety, health, happiness, and well-being of society, but earn less than he does, Buffett says:

"This society provides me with enormous rewards for what I bring to this society."[491]

~

"I personally think that society is responsible for a very significant percentage of what I've earned. If you stick me down in the middle of Bangladesh or Peru or someplace, you'll find out how much this talent is going to produce in the wrong kind of soil. I will be struggling 30 years later. I work in a market

~

"We like to buy businesses. We don't like to sell, and we expect the relationships to last a lifetime."[482]

~

"Most of our large stock positions are going to be held for many years, and the scorecard on our investment decisions will be provided by business results over that period, and not by prices on any given day. Just as it would be foolish to focus unduly on short-term prospects when acquiring an entire company, we think it equally unsound to become mesmerized by the prospective near-term earnings when purchasing small pieces of a company, i.e., marketable common stocks."[483]

~

Not only does Buffett invest for the long haul, he hopes Berkshire Hathaway shareholders will keep their shares as long as possible:

"If I had a club, or if I (were) preaching at a church, I would not measure my success by how frequent the turnover of the congregation was or (what) the club membership would be. I would really like the idea that nobody wanted to leave their seats so that there wouldn't be a seat available for anybody else."[484]

~

A corporate acquisition can be thought of this way:

"It's a little like a romance for a while. You spend some time with them, and you know, you have your first date. And then, finally, the big moment comes. The next day, do you want to start thinking about if somebody offers me 2X for this or 3X for this, would I sell it?"[485]

~

Buffett says he's a "Rip Van Winkle" investor:

"My favorite time frame for holding a stock is forever."[486]

~

TO SUM UP

"Stocks are simple. All you do is buy shares in a great business for less than the business is intrinsically worth, with managers of the highest integrity and ability. Then you own those shares forever."[487]

~

Or, Buffett says, you can follow Will Rogers. Rogers said to study the markets carefully before buying a stock; then:

"When the stock doubles, sell it."

What if the stock doesn't double?

"If it doesn't double, don't buy it."[488]

~

AND WHEN YOU'VE BECOME WEAL FOLLOWING IN THE FOOTSTEPS (BUFFETT, PAY YOUR DUES TO SOC

One of the qualities that makes Buffett, his fri his colleagues unique is their attitude regardi responsibility to others with whom they share th

INVESTING IS ONE WAY OF CONTRIBUTING TO THE PUBLIC WELL-BEING

"Large gains in real capital, invested in m production facilities, are required to produce gains in economic well-being. Great labor avail ity, great consumer wants, and great governm promises will lead to nothing but great frustrat without continuous creation and employment expensive new capital assets throughout industr That's an equation understood by Russians as we as Rockefellers. And it's one that has been applie with stunning success in West Germany and Japan High capital-accumulation rates have enabled those countries to achieve gains in living standards at rates far exceeding ours, even though we have enjoyed much the superior position in energy."[489]

~

Although some investors profit, leveraged buyouts aren't always good for society. For one thing, substituting debt for equity reduces taxes the company pays, which finance social programs.

system that happens to reward what I do very well—disproportionately well. Mike Tyson, too. If you can knock a guy out in 10 seconds and earn $10 million for it, this world will pay a lot for that. If you can bat .360, the world will pay a lot for that. If you're a marvelous teacher, this world won't pay a lot for it. If you are a terrific nurse, this world will not pay a lot for it. Now, am I going to try to come up with some comparable worth system that somehow (re)distributes that. No, I don't think you can do that. But I do think that when you're treated enormously well by this market system, where in effect the market system showers the ability to buy goods and services on you because of some peculiar talent—maybe your adenoids are a certain way, so you can sing and everybody will pay you enormous sums to be on television or whatever—I think society has a big claim on that."492

~

"I don't have a problem with guilt about money. The way I see it is that my money represents an enormous number of claim checks on society. It's like I have these little pieces of paper that I can turn into consumption. If I wanted to, I could hire 10,000 people to do nothing but paint my picture every day for the rest of my life. And the GNP would go up. But the utility of the product would be zilch, and I would be keeping those 10,000 people from doing AIDS research, or teaching, or nursing. I don't do

165

that, though. I don't use very many of those claim checks. There's nothing material I want very much. And I'm going to give virtually all of those claim checks to charity when my wife and I die."[493]

~

Buffett offered another example of how "claim checks" work, in a eulogy he wrote for Omaha real estate developer Peter Kiewit (Buffett admired Kiewit because he saved his claim checks, leaving much of his $200 million estate to charity):

"In essence, one who spends less than he earns is accumulating 'claim checks' for future use. At some later date, he may reverse the procedure and consume more than he earns by cashing some of the accumulated claim checks. Or he may pass them on to others—either during his lifetime by gifts, or upon his death by bequest.

"(William Randolph) Hearst, for example, used up many of his claim checks in building and maintaining San Simeon. Just as the pharaohs did when building pyramids, Hearst commanded massive amounts of labor and material away from other societal purposes in order to satisfy his personal consumption desires.

"An army of servants catering to his personal whims—such as the employee in San Luis Obispo who spent much of a lifetime hauling ice daily to the bears in the private zoo—was unavailable to produce other goods and services useful to society in general."[494]

~

Buffett's friend Bill Gates says he expects to run Microsoft until about 2007, then promises to focus on how to give his fortune away. Buffett expects that Gates will return some claim check to society:

"He will spend time, at some point, thinking about the impact his philanthropy can have. He is too imaginative to just do conventional gifts."[495]

SAY THANKS

Though the Buffetts will leave the largest charitable foundation in the world when they die, critics complain that he doesn't contribute enough to good causes while he is living. Buffett did please the community by investing $1.25 million in the Omaha Royals in 1991 to keep the AAA baseball team from leaving town. (Some people view this as an investment, but former owner of the San Diego Padres Joan Kroc says a baseball club is more like a hobby for most owners.) Buffett also established the Alice Buffett Outstanding Teacher Awards in Omaha, named for his Aunt Alice, who was a local teacher. While the substantial cash awards may inspire better teaching, Buffett says the grants are "more a way of saying thanks than a prod." Teachers get the money to spend as they wish with no strings attached.

He adds:

"The public school teacher is probably the most under-compensated and under-appreciated person in the public arena."[496]

~

"The public school system is the most important institution in our democracy. But as important as it is, it is just as fragile. When we have an outstanding system like Omaha's, we should do everything we can to help it."[497]

NOTE: One reason the Buffetts are criticized for not making enough donations is because their giving is targeted and done quietly. Susan Buffett who is president of the Buffett Foundation says, "Our foundation is focused on population (problems), and my other giving is very personal."[498]

PAY YOUR TAXES
AND DON'T COMPLAIN

When explaining that Berkshire paid federal taxes of $390 million in 1993, Buffett said:

"Charlie and I have absolutely no complaints about these taxes. We work in a market-based economy that rewards our efforts far more bountifully than it does the efforts of others whose output is of equal or greater benefit to society. Taxation should, and does, partially redress this inequity. But we remain extraordinarily well treated."[499]

Buffett has written that a 100 percent tax on profits from the sale of a security that is held for less than a year—applied to everyone, including institutional investors—would make the United States more competitive. By forcing investors to hold their shares longer, the industry would be more stable.

"We talk a lot about competing in a world economy against foriegn decision makers who operate with a business horizon of decades. Why not try pushing our own horizon out at least a year?"[500]

∼

As often is the case, Munger's position is similar to Buffett's, except that it reflects his Republican leanings. Munger explains: "I like a certain amount of social intervention (taxes, laws, etc.) that takes some of the inequity out of capitalism, but I abhor any system that allows rewarding fakes."

For example, Munger says he dislikes worker's compensation for job-related injuries and disabilities because it is difficult to sort out the bogus claims.[501]

THE LAST WORD

Publishers, bookstore owners, investors, fans, and imitators have long awaited a book that Buffett himself will write. Buffett says he has been discussing the project with a co-author—*Fortune* editor and writer Carol J. Loomis—since 1973.

"The big hang-up—aside from a normal heavy dose of procrastination—is that if I ever do a book, I want it to be useful," he wrote in a 1989 letter to me. "This means good ideas—and ideas that have not already been presented. My most important ideas are straight from Ben Graham, and he stated them far better than I ever could.

"If the book is to be biographical, I believe I should wait a while. I am enough of an optimist to hope that the most interesting chapters are yet to come."[502]

Though Buffett seems as healthy and energetic as ever, there is some indication that Warren and Carol are indeed at work on *the* book. I, for one, can hardly wait to read more of the wise and witty words of Warren Buffett.

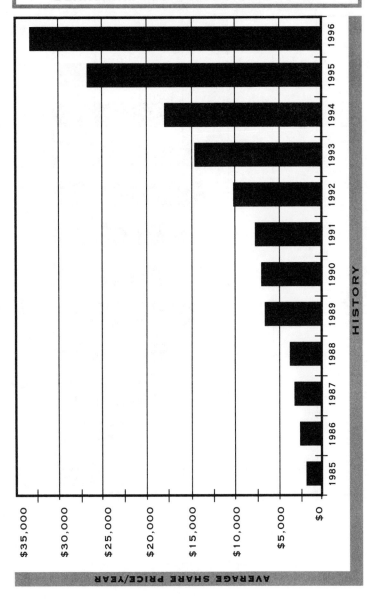

BERKSHIRE HATHAWAY SHARE PRICE

HISTORY

AVERAGE SHARE PRICE/YEAR

171

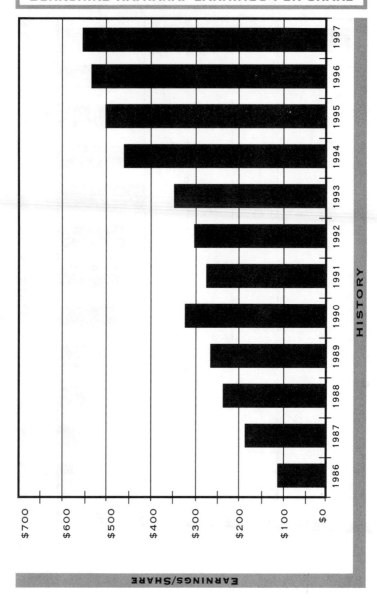

BERKSHIRE HATHAWAY EARNINGS PER SHARE

HISTORY

EARNINGS/SHARE

172

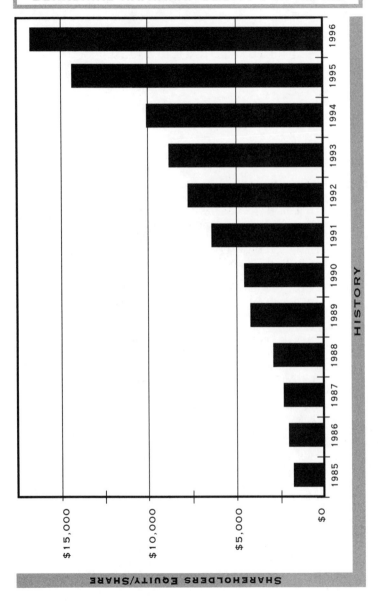

BERKSHIRE HATHAWAY EQUITY PER SHARE

SHAREHOLDERS EQUITY/SHARE

HISTORY

173

ENDNOTES

1. "The New Establishment 50," *Vanity Fair*, October, 1995, p. 280.

2. "In from the Cold," *The Economist*, May 23, 1992, p. 86.

3. R. Hutchings Vernon, "The Warren and Charlie Show: Notes from the 1996 Berkshire Hathaway Annual Meeting," May 6, 1996.

4. "What I Learned from Warren Buffett," Bill Gates, *Harvard Business Review*, January/February 1996. Copyright 1995, Microsoft Corp.

5. Bob Reilly, "The Richest Man in America," *USWest*, Autumn, 1987, p. 2.

6. L. J. Davis, "Buffett Takes Stock," *The New York Times Magazine*, April 1, 1990, p. 16. (Modified later by Buffett letter to author.)

7. Bob Reilly, "The Richest Man in America," *USWest*, Autumn, 1987, p. 2.

8. L. J. Davis, "Buffett Takes Stock," *The New York Times Magazine*, April 1, 1990, p. 16.

9. Bob Reilly, "The Richest Man in America," *USWest*, Autumn, 1987, p. 2.

10. Robert McMorris, "Unparsimonious Billionaire Puzzled by Warren Buffett," *Omaha World-Herald*, December 3, 1987, p. B1.

11. Linda Grant, "Striking Out at Wall Street," *U.S. News & World Report*, June 20, 1994, p. 58.

12. William D. Orr's *First Gentleman's Cookbook*, (Lincoln, IVb., William D. Orr, 1987) p.178.

13. Berkshire Hathaway annual meeting, Omaha, 1992.

14. Ann Hughey, "Omaha's Plain Dealer," *Newsweek*, April 1, 1985, p. 56.

15. *Forbes 400*, October 24, 1988, p. 155.

16. *The New York Times*, May 20, 1990, as reported in Andrew Kilpatrick, *Of Permanent Value: The Story of Waren Buffett*, (Birmingham: AKPE, 1994) p. 568.

17. Robert Dorr, "Investor Warren Buffett Views Making Money as 'Big Game,'" *Omaha World-Herald*, March 3, 1985, p. 1.

18. Andrew Kilpatrick, *Of Permanent Value: The Story of Warren Buffett*, (Birmingham: AKPE, 1994) p. 81.

19. David C. Churbuck, "Games Grown-ups Play," *Forbes*, December 19, 1994, p. 308.

20. Video prepared for and played at the Berkshire Hathaway annual meeting, 1996.

21. "Billionaires," *Forbes 400*, October 18, 1993, p. 112.

22. Berkshire Hathaway annual meeting, Omaha, May 1, 1995.

23. L. J. Davis, "Buffett Takes Stock," *The New York Times Magazine*, April 1, 1990, p. 16.

24. Warren Buffett, 1986 Capital Cities/ABC management conference.

25. Berkshire Hathaway annual meeting, Omaha, May 21, 1984.

26. Warren Buffett, "Oil Discovered in Hell," *Investment Decisions*, May, 1985, p. 22.

27. Alan Gersten, "Buffett Faces Shareholders," *Omaha World-Herald*, May 21, 1986, p. 27.

28. Berkshire Hathaway annual meeting, Omaha, April 29, 1991.

29. Sue Baggarly interview with Warren Buffett, WOWT-TV, Channel 6, October 14, 1993.

30. Jim Rasmussen, "Billionaire Talks Strategy with Students," *Omaha World-Herald*, January 2, 1994, p. 17S.

31. Andrew Kilpatrick, *Of Permanent Value: The Story of Warren Buffett*, (Birmingham: AKPE, 1994) p. 488.

32. Robert G. Hagstrom Jr., *The Warren Buffett Way*, (New York, John Wiley & Sons, Inc.,1994) p. 22.

33. Berkshire Hathaway annual meeting, Omaha, May 1, 1995.

34. Berkshire Hathaway annual meeting, Omaha, 1991.

35. Carol J. Loomis, "The Inside Story of Warren Buffett," *Fortune*, April 11, 1988, p. 26.

36. Warren Buffett speech at Emory Business College, November, 1989 (as reported by Andrew Kilpatrick in *Of Permanent Value: The Story of Warren Buffett*, Birmingham: AKPE, 1994).

37. Patricia E. Bauer, "The Convictions of a Long-Distance Investor," *Channels*, November 1986, p. 22.

38. *Forbes 400*, October 28, 1985, p. 118.

39. Bob Reilly, "The Richest Man in America," *USWest*, Autumn 1987, p. 2.

40. Patricia Bauer, "The Convictions of a Long-Distance Investor," *Channels*, November, 1986, p. 22.

41. John Rothchild, "How Smart Is Warren Buffett?" *Time*, April 3, 1995, p. 54.

42. Robert Dorr, "Buffetts Have become 1st Billionaires in State," *Omaha World-Herald*, July 28, 1985, p. 1.

43. Alan Gersten, "Buffett Ranks 8th as 'Biggest Stakeholder,'" *Omaha World-Herald*, July 16, 1986, p. 29.

44. "Billionaires," *Forbes 400*, October 18, 1993, p. 112.

45. Art Buchwald, "The Burden of Being Second Best," *The Los Angeles Times*, Thursday, July 20, 1995, p. E4.

46. Roger Lowenstein, *Buffett: The Making of an American Capitalist*, (New York: Random House, 1995) p. 111.

47. Kathy McCormack, "Buffett's Crisis Control: Lay It Out as You See It." *San Diego Union*, Associated Press, September 3, 1992. (Modified later by Buffett letter to author.)

48. Liz Smith, "Lifestyles' Catches Elusive Billionaire," *New Jersey Star Ledger*, November 4, 1992.

49. Mark M. Colodny, "Warren Buffett's Tuffest Critic," *Fortune*, June 3, 1991, p. 211.

50. Andrew Kilpatrick, *Of Permanent Value: The Story of Warren Buffett*, (Birmingham: AKPE, 1994) p. 237.

51. "Warren Buffett Talks Business," PBSTV program produced by the University of North Carolina, Center for Public Television, Chapel Hill, 1995.

52. Ibid.

53. "The New Establishment 50." *Vanity Fair*, October, 1996, p. 280.

54. Roger Lowenstein, *Buffett: The Making of an American Capitalist*, (New York: Random House, 1995) p. 46.

55. Linda Grant, "Striking Out at Wall Street," *U.S. News & World Report*, June 20, 1994, p. 58.

56. John Train, *The Money Masters*, (New York: Harper & Row, 1980) p. 5.

57. Brett Duval Fromson, "Are These the New Warren Buffetts?" *Fortune, 1990 Investor's Guide*, p. 98.

58. Bob Reilly, "The Richest Man in America," *USWest*, Autumn, 1987, p. 2.

59. Jim Rasmussen, "Billionaire Talks Strategy with Students," *Omaha World-Herald*, January 2, 1994, p. 17S.

60. Beth Botts, et al., "The Corn-fed Capitalist," *Regardie's*, February, 1986.

61. Interview with author, May 25, 1993.

62. Interview with Sue Baggarly, WOWT-TV, Omaha, October 14, 1993.

63. Berkshire Hathaway annual meeting, Omaha, 1994.

64. Ron Suskind, "Legend Revisited: Warren Buffett's Aura as Folksy Sage Masks Tough, Polished Man." *The Wall Street Journal*, Nov. 8, 1991, p. 1.

65. Andrew Kilpatrick, *Of Permanent Value: The Story of Warren Buffett*, (Birmingham: AKPE, 1994) p. 65.

66. "Investor Buffett's Speculations Reap Artistic Returns," *Omaha World-Herald*, May 30, 1985, p. 1.

67. Berkshire Hathaway annual meeting, Omaha, May 6, 1996.

68. Linda Grant, "The $4-Billion Regular Guy," *The Los Angeles Times*, Sunday, April 7, 1991, p. 36.

69. Berkshire Hathaway annual meeting, Omaha, 1991.

70. From a video made for and shown at the 1996 Berkshire Hathaway annual meeting.

71. Andrew Kilpatrick, *Of Permanent Value: The Story of Warren Buffett*, (Birmingham: AKPE, 1994) p. 72.

72. Warren Buffett speech, New York Society of Security Analysts, December 6, 1994.

73. Robert Lenzner, "Warren Buffett's Idea of Heaven: I don't have to work with people I don't like," *Forbes 400*, October 18, 1993, p. 112.

74. Robert McMorris, "Leila Buffett Basks in Value of Son's Life, Not Fortune," *Omaha World-Herald*, May 16, 1987, p. 17.

75. Patricia E. Bauer, "The Convictions of a Long-Distance Investor," *Channels*, November, 1986, p. 22.

76. Robert Lenzner, "Warren Buffett's Idea of Heaven: I don't have to work with people I don't like," *Forbes 400*, October 18, 1993, p. 40.

77. Robynn Tysver, "Warren Buffett Hits Campaign Trail," *The San Diego Union-Tribune*, Associated Press, October 16, 1994, p. I-1.

78. "The Money Men: How Omaha Beats Wall Street," *Forbes*, November 1, 1969, p. 82.

79. Warren Buffett, "What We Can Learn from Phil Fisher," *Forbes*, October 19, 1987, p. 40.

80. Alan Deutschman, "Bill Gates' Next Challenge," *Fortune*, December 28, 1992, p. 31.

81. Ibid.

82. Interview with author, Omaha, May 25, 1993.

83. SEC File No. HO-784, Blue Chip Stamps, et al./Warren Buffett, letter to Charles N. Huggins, December 13, 1972.

84. From a video prepared for and shown at the 1996 Berkshire Hathaway annual meeting.

85. Warren Buffett, "The 3 Percent Solution," *The Washington Post*, September 14, 1993, p. A21.

86. *Forbes 400*, October 19, 1992, p. 93.

87. Berkshire Hathaway annual meeting, Omaha, 1992.

88. John Huey, "The World's Best Brand," *Fortune*, May 31, 1993, p. 44.

89. Carol J. Loomis, "The Inside Story of Warren Buffett," *Fortune*, April 11, 1988, p. 26.

90. Berkshire Hathaway annual meeting, Omaha, 1987.

91. Carol J. Loomis, "The Inside Story of Warren Buffett," *Fortune*, April 11, 1988, p. 26.

92. Robert Dorr, "Furniture Mart Handshake Deal," *Omaha World-Herald*, September 15, 1993, p. E1.

93. Beth Botts, et al., "The Corn-fed Capitalist," *Regardie's*, February 1986, p. 53.

94. Ibid., p. 45.

95. "Warren Buffett Talks Business," The University of North Carolina, Center for Public Television, Chapel Hill, 1995.

96. Bernice Kanner, "Aw Shucks, It's Warren Buffett," *New York Magazine*, April 22, 1985, p. 52.

97. Michael Kelly, "Mrs. B. Cruises into Year 100." *Omaha World-Herald*, December 17, 1992, p. 17SF.

98. Linda Grant, "The $4-Billion Regular Guy," *The Los Angeles Times Magazine*, Sunday, April 7, 1991.

99. Bernice Kanner, "Aw Shucks, It's Warren Buffett," *New York Magazine*, April 22, 1985, p. 52.

100. John R. Hayes, "The Oversight Was Understandable," *Forbes*, April 26, 1993.

101. Andrew Kilpatrick, *Of Permanent Value: The Story of Warren Buffett*, (Birmingham: AKPE, 1994) p. 429.

102. Bob Reilly, "The Richest Man in America," *USWest*, Autumn 1987, p. 2.

103. Ibid.

104. Adam Smith, *Supermoney*, (New York: Random House, 1972) p. 198.

105. L. J. Davis, "Buffett Takes Stock," *The New York Times Magazine*, April 1, 1990, p. 16.

106. Robert Dorr, "Ex-Omahan Traded Law for Board Room," *Omaha World-Herald*, August 31, 1977, p. B1.

107. Carol J. Loomis, "The Inside Story of Warren Buffett," *Fortune*, April 11, 1988, p. 26.

108. Robert Lenzner and David S. Fondiller, "The Not-So-Silent Partner," *Forbes*, January 22, 1996, p. 78.

109. Berkshire Hathaway annual meeting, Omaha, 1996.

110. John Train, *The Midas Touch*, (New York: Harper & Row, 1987) p. 70.

111. Andrew Kilpatrick, *Of Permanent Value: The Story of Warren Buffett*, (Birmingham: AKPE, 1994) p. 489.

112. Robert Lenzner, "Warren Buffett's Idea of Heaven: I don't have to work with people I don't like," *Forbes 400*, October 18, 1993.

113. Robert Lenzner and David S. Fondiller, "Meet Charlie Munger," *Forbes*, January 22, 1996, p. 78.

114. Brett Duval Fromson, "And Now, a Look at the Old One," *Fortune, 1990 Investor's Guide*, p. 98.

115. Robert Lenzner, "Warren Buffett's Idea of Heaven: I don't have to work with people I don't like," *Forbes 400*, October 18, 1993, p. 40.

116. Robert Dorr, "Buffett's Right-hand Man," *Omaha World-Herald*, August 10, 1986, p.1.

117. Robert Lenzner and David S. Fondiller, "Meet Charlie Munger," *Forbes*, January 22, 1996, p.78.

118. Berkshire Hathaway annual meeting, Omaha, May 1, 1995.

119. Berkshire Hathaway annual meeting, Omaha, 1996. (Modified later by Buffett letter to author.)

120. Roger Lowenstein, *Buffett: The Making of an American Capitalist*, (New York: Random House, 1995) p. 75.

121. Robert Dorr, "Ex-Omahan Traded Law for Board Room," *Omaha World-Herald*, August 3, 1977, p. B1.

122. Carol J. Loomis, "The Inside Story of Warren Buffett," *Fortune*, April 11, 1988, p. 26.

123. Andrew Kilpatrick, *Of Permanent Value: The Story of Warren Buffett*, (Birmingham: AKPE, 1994) p. 98.

124. Ron Suskind, "Legend Revisited: Warren Buffett's Aura as Folksy Sage Masks Tough, Polished Man." *The Wall Street Journal*, November 8, 1991, p. 1.

125. Robynn Tysver, "Warren Buffett Hits Campaign Trail," *The San Diego Union-Tribune*, Associated Press, October 16, 1994, p. I-1.

126. Robert Lenzner, "Warren Buffett's Idea of Heaven: I don't have to work with people I don't like," *Forbes 400*, October 18, 1993, p. 40.

127. "Warren Buffett Talks Business," The University of North Carolina, Center for Public Television, Chapel Hill, 1995.

128. Michael Kelly, "Susie Funny Like Her Dad," *Omaha World-Herald*, May 26, 1996, p. B1.

129. Bob Reilly, "The Richest Man in America," *USWest*, Autumn, 1987, p. 2.

130. Berkshire Hathaway annual meeting, Omaha, April 27, 1992.

131. *Outstanding Investor Digest*, March 6, 1989, p. 4.

132. As said to Bruce Marks, 1996 Berkshire Hathaway annual meeting.

133. Andrew Kilpatrick, *Of Permanent Value: The Story of Warren Buffett*, (Birmingham: APKE, 1994) p. 508.

134. Beth Botts et al., "The Corn-fed Capitalist," *Regardies*, February, 1986, p. 45.

135. Ron Suskind, "Legend Revisited: Warren Buffett's Aura as Folksy Sage Masks Tough, Polished Man." *The Wall Street Journal*, November 8, 1991, p. 1.

136. Linda Grant, "The $4-Billion Regular Guy," *The Los Angeles Times*, Sunday, April 7, 1991, p. 36.

137. Adam Smith, "The Modest Billionaire," *Esquire*, October 1988, p. 103.

138. Michael Kelly, "Susie Funny Like Her Dad," *Omaha World-Herald*, May 26, 1996, p. B1.

139. Robert Dorr, "Investor Warren Buffett Views Making Money as 'Big Game,'" *Omaha World-Herald*, March 24, 1985, p. 1.

140. Ken Kurson, "The Buffett with a Bullet" *Worth*, April, 1996, p. 25.

141. Tom Ineck, "A Little 'Dance' Music Lifts Son of Omaha Billionaire," *The Lincoln Journal and Star*, August 8, 1991, p. 11.

142. Linda Grant, "The $4-Billion Regular Guy," *The Los Angeles Times*, Sunday, April 7, 1991, p. 36.

143. Robert McMorris, "Leila Buffett Basks in Value of Son's Life, Not Fortune," *Omaha World-Herald*, May 16, 1987, p. 17.

144. Ibid.

145. Ibid.

146. Ron Suskind, "Legend Revisited: Warren Buffett's Aura as Folksy Sage Masks Tough, Polished Man." *The Wall Street Journal*, November 8, 1991, p. 1.

147. *Outstanding Investor Digest*, March 6, 1989, p. 8.

148. *Outstanding Investor Digest*, June 23, 1989, p. 16.

149. John Train, *The New Money Masters*, (New York: Harper & Row, 1989) p. 55.

150. Bill Gates, *The Road Ahead*, (New York: Viking Press, 1995) p. 240–241.

151. John Train, *The Midas Touch*, (New York, Harper & Row, 1987) p. 2.

152. David Elsner, "It Works: Buying $1 for 40 cents," *Chicago Tribune*, December 8, 1985, p. 1.

153. Linda Grant, "The $4-Billion Regular Guy," *The Los Angeles Times*, April 7, 1991, p. 36.

154. Carol J. Loomis, "The Inside Story of Warren Buffett," *Fortune*, April 11, 1988, p. 26.

155. Bernice Kanner, "Aw Shucks, it's Warren Buffett," *New York Magazine*, April 22, 1983, p. 52.

156. Carol J. Loomis, "The Inside Story of Warren Buffett," *Fortune*, April 11, 1988, p. 26.

157. Ron Suskind, "Legend Revisited: Warren Buffett's Aura as Folksy Sage Masks Tough, Polished Man." *The Wall Street Journal*, November 8, 1991. p. 1.

158. Andrew Kilpatrick, *Of Permanent Value: The Story of Warren Buffett*, (Birmingham: AKPE, 1994) p. 40.

159. Ron Suskind, "Legend Revisited: Warren Buffett's Aura as Folksy Sage Masks Tough, Polished Man." *The Wall Street Journal*, November 8, 1991, p. 1.

160. Ibid.

161. Robert Dorr, "Investor Warren Buffett Views Making Money as 'Big Game,'" *Omaha World-Herald*, March 24, 1985, p. 1.

162. Al Pagel, "Susie Sings for More than Her Supper," *Omaha World-Herald*, April 17, 1977.

163. Ibid.

164. Ibid.

165. Robert McMorris, "Unparsimonius Billionaire Puzzled by Warren Buffett," *Omaha World-Herald*, December 3, 1987. (Modified later by Buffett letter to author.)

166. Robert McMorris, "Leila Buffett Basks in Value of Son's Life, Not Fortune," *Omaha World-Herald*, May 16, 1987, p. 17.

167. Sue Baggarly interview, WOWT-TV, Omaha, October 14, 1993.

168. Linda Sandler, "Buffett's Savior Role Lands Him Deals Others Can't Get," *The Wall Street Journal*, August 14, 1989, p. C1.

169. Robert McMorris, "Unparsimonious Billionaire Puzzled by Warren Buffett," *Omaha World-Herald*, December 3, 1987.

170. Ron Suskind, "Legend Revisited: Warren Buffett's Aura as Folksy Sage Masks Tough, Polished Man." *The Wall Street Journal*, November 8, 1991, p. 1.

171. Michael Lewis, "The Temptation of St. Warren," *The New Republic*, February 17, 1992, p. 23.

172. Warren Buffett interview with the author, Omaha, May 25, 1993.

173. Speech given by Waren Buffett at Columbia Graduate School of Business, October 27, 1993.

174. Bob Reilly, "The Richest Man in America," *USWest*, Autumn 1987, p. 2.

175. Roger Lowenstein, *Buffett: The Making of an American Capitalist*, (New York: Random House, 1995) p. 20.

176. L. J. Davis, "Buffett Takes Stock," *The New York Times Magazine*, April 1, 1990, p. 16.

177. Robynn Tysver, "Warren Buffett Hits Campaign Trail," *The San Diego Union-Tribune*, Associated Press, October 16, 1994, p. I-1.

178. L. J. Davis, "Buffett Takes Stock," *The New York Times Magazine*, April 1, 1990, p. 16.

179. Robert Dorr, "Investor Warren Buffett Views Making Money as 'Big Game,'" *Omaha World-Herald*, March 24, 1985.

180. "Eye," *Women's Wear Daily*, October 10, 1985, p. 10.

181. *Forbes 400*, October 22, 1990, p. 122.

182. Jonathan Liang, "Investor Who Piled Up $100 Million in the '60s Piles Up Firms Today," *The Wall Street Journal*, March 31, 1977, p. 27.

183. Berkshire Hathaway annual meeting, Omaha, 1988.

184. Linda Grant, "The $4-Billion Regular Guy," *The Los Angeles Times Magazine*, April 7, 1991, p. 34.

185. "How Omaha Beats Wall Street," *Forbes*, November 1, 1969, p. 82. (Modified later by Buffett letter to author.)

186. Bernice Kanner, "Aw Shucks, It's Warren Buffett," *New York Magazine*, April 22, 1985, p. 52.

187. John Train, *The Midas Touch*, (New York: Harper & Row, 1987) p. 5.

188. L. J. Davis, "Buffett Takes Stock," *The New York Times Magazine*, April 1, 1990, p. 16.

189. "Expert on Investing Plans to Slow Down," *Omaha World-Herald*, February 25, 1968, p. 1. (Modified later by Buffett letter to author.)

190. Adam Smith, *Supermoney*, (New York: Random House, 1972) p. 182.

191. David A. Vise and Steve Coll, "Buffett-watchers Follow Lead of Omaha's Long-term Stock Investor," *The Washington Post*, October 2, 1987, p. D1

192. "How to Live with a Billion," *Fortune*, September 11, 1989, p. 50.

193. L. J. Davis, "Buffett Takes Stock," *The New York Times Magazine*, April 1, 1990, p. 16.

194. Jim Rasmussen, "Billionaire Talks Strategy with Students," *Omaha World-Herald*, January 2, 1994, p. 17S.

195. Ibid. p. 24.

196. "ABC Affiliates Hear Network's Fall Strategy," *Broadcasting*, June 9, 1986, p. 22.

197. "Warren Buffett Talks Business," The University of North Carolina, Center for Public Television, Chapel Hill, 1995.

198. Larry van Dyne, "The Bottom Line on Katharine Graham," *The Washingtonian*, December 1985, p. 204.

199. Patricia E. Bauer, "The Convictions of a Long-Distance Investor," *Channels*, November 1986, p. 22.

200. Ibid, p. 24.

201. Berkshire Hathaway annual meeting, Omaha, 1991.

202. Patricia E. Bauer, "The Convictions of a Long-Distance Investor," *Channels*, November, 1986, p. 22.

203. Andrew Kilpatrick, *Of Permanent Value: The Story of Warren Buffett*," (Birmingham: AKPE, 1994) p. 102.

204. Ann Hughey, "Omaha's Plain Dealer," *Newsweek*, April 1, 1985, p. 56.

205. Jim Rasmussen, "Brother, Can You Spare a Million?" *Omaha World-Herald*, October 10, 1993, p. 1A.

206. Berkshire Hathaway annual meeting, Omaha, 1989.

207. Roger Lowenstein, *Buffett: The Making of an American Capitalist*, (New York: Random House, 1995) p. 286.

208. *Forbes 400*, October 19, 1992, p. 93.

209. Robert Dorr, "Buffett Plans to Shut Down Finance Firm," *Omaha World-Herald*, June 2, 1969.

210. "Buffett Report Makes *Times* List," *Omaha World-Herald*, April 22, 1985, p. B1

211. "Warren Buffett Talks Business," The University of North Carolina, Center for Public Television, Chapel Hill, 1995.

212. Ibid.

213. Gordon Matthews, "Wells' Stock Continues to Climb on Speculation Buffett Is Buying," *American Banker*, November 10, 1992, p. 16.

214. "Omahan Mum on His Ideas for Grinnell's Investments," *Omaha World-Herald*, July 18, 1980.

215. Salomon Inc.: A report by the chairman on the company's standing and outlook. *The New York Times*, Thursday, October 29, 1991.

216. Ibid.

217. Robert Dorr, "Early Faith Made Many 'Buffett Millionaires,'" *Omaha World-Herald*, May 5, 1986, p. 1

218. Judith H. Dobrzynski, "Warren's World," *Business Week*, May 10, 1993, p. 30.

219. Salomon Inc.: A report by the chairman on the company's standing and outlook, *The New York Times*, Thursday, October 29, 1991, p. 12.

220. "Now Hear This," *Fortune*, January 10, 1994, p. 20.

221. John Train, *The Money Masters*, (New York: Harper & Row, 1980) p. 23.

222. *Outstanding Investor Digest*, May 24, 1991.

223. Carol J. Loomis, "The Inside Story of Warren Buffett," *Fortune*, April 11, 1988, p. 26.

224. "Warren Buffett Talks Business," The University of North Carolina, Center for Public Television, Chapel Hill, 1995.

225. Robert G. Hagstrom Jr., *The Warren Buffett Way*, (New York: John Wiley & Sons Inc. 1994) p. v.

226. Robert Lenzner, "Warren Buffett's Idea of Heaven: I don't have to work with people I don't like," *Forbes 400*, October 18, 1993, p. 40.

227. Carol J. Loomis, "The Inside Story of Warren Buffett," *Fortune*, April 11, 1988, p. 26.

228. Berkshire Hathaway annual meeting, Omaha, April 29, 1991.

229. Ibid.

230. Berkshire Hathaway annual meeting, Omaha, 1993.

231. Berkshire Hathaway annual meeting, Omaha, April 27, 1992.

232. Berkshire Hathaway annual meeting, Omaha, April 29, 1991.

233. Alan Gersten, "Buffett Faces Shareholders," *Omaha World-Herald*, May 21, 1986, p. 27.

234. Berkshire Hathaway annual meeting, Omaha, 1994.

235. Salomon Brothers annual meeting, New York, May, 1992.

236. Interview with Linda O'Bryon, *Nightly Business Report*, May 6, 1996.

237. Carol J. Loomis, "The Inside Story of Warren Buffett," *Fortune*, April 11, 1988, p. 26.

238. "The Forbes Four Hundred Billionaires," *Forbes 400*, October 27, 1986.

239. Warren Buffett speech, New York Society of Security Analysts, December 6, 1994.

240. Robert Lenzner, "Warren Buffett's Idea of Heaven: I don't have to work with people I don't like," *Forbes 400*, October 18, 1993, p. 40.

241. Berkshire Hathaway annual meeting, Omaha, 1988.

242. Warren E. Buffett, "How Inflation Swindles the Investor," *Fortune*, May 5, 1977, p. 250.

243. Ibid.

244. "Warren Buffett Is in Stocks Anyway," *Fortune*, May, 1977, p. 253.

245. Warren Buffett, "Investing in Equity Markets," quoted in Columbia University Business School, transcript of a seminar held March 13, 1985, p. 23.

246. Robert Dorr, "Investor Warren Buffett Views Making Money as 'Big Game,'" *Omaha World-Herald*, March 24, 1985.

247. Adam Smith, *Supermoney*, (New York: Random House, 1972) p. 181.

248. L. J. Davis, "Buffett Takes Stock," *The New York Times Magazine*, April 1, 1990, p. 16.

249. Warren Buffett correspondence to Benjamin Graham, July 17, 1970.

250. Warren Buffett speech, New York Society of Security Analysts, December 6, 1994.

251. Buffett interview with the author, Omaha, May 25, 1993.

252. Berkshire Hathaway annual meeting, Omaha, April 27, 1992.

253. Warren Buffett speech, New York Society of Security Analysts, December 6, 1994.

254. Berkshire Hathaway annual meeting, Omaha, May 1, 1995.

255. Warren Buffett speech, New York Society of Security Analysts, December 6, 1994.

256. Benjamin Graham, *The Intelligent Investor* (New York: Harper & Row, 1973) p. 216.

257. Benjamin Graham and David Dodd, *Security Analysis,* (New York: McGraw-Hill, 1940) p. 43.

258. Benjamin Graham, "Current Problems in Security Analysis," transcripts of lectures, September 1946–February 1947, New York Institute of Finance, p. 102.

259. Robert Lenzner, "Warren Buffett's Idea of Heaven: I don't have to work with people I don't Like," *Forbes 400*, October 18, 1993, p. 40.

260. Anthony Bianco, "Why Warren Buffett Is Breaking His Own Rules," *Business Week*, April 15, 1985, p. 134.

261. William Ruane, interview with the author, June 1993.

262. Warren Buffett speech, New York Society of Security Analysts, December 6, 1994.

263. Ibid.

264. Patricia E. Bauer, "The Convictions of a Long-Distance Investor," *Channels*, November 1986, p. 22.

265. Warren Buffett interview with the author, Omaha, May 25, 1993.

266. Warren Buffett Interview with the author, May 25, 1993, and interview with Charles Brandes, also in May 1993.

267. Terence P. Pare, "Yes, You Can Beat the Market," *Fortune*, April 3, 1995, p. 69 (Modified later by Buffett letter to author.)

268. L. J. Davis, "Buffett Takes Stock," *The New York Times Magazine*, April 1, 1990. p. 16.

269. Linda Grant, "The $4-Billion Regular Guy," *The Los Angeles Times Magazine*, April 7, 1991, p. 36.

270. Berkshire Hathaway annual meeting, Omaha, May 6, 1996.

271. Ibid.

272. Leah Nathans Spiro and David Greising, "Why Amex Wooed Warren Buffett," *Business Week*, August 19, 1991, p. 97.

273. Anthony Simpson, *The Midas Touch*, (New York: Dutton, 1990) p. 79.

274. "Buffett Listed by Fortune with Wall Street Winners," *Omaha World-Herald*, July 31, 1983, quoting from *Fortune* magazine, August 8, 1983.

275. "Look at All Those Beautiful, Scantily Clad Girls Out There," *Forbes*, November 1, 1974.

276. Patricia E. Bauer, "The Convictions of a Long-Distance Investor," *Channels*, November, 1986, p. 22.

277. *Forbes 400*, October 1, 1985, p. 82.

278. Berkshire Hathaway annual meeting, Omaha, 1994.

279. Ibid.

280. "Faces Behind the Figures," *Forbes*, January 4, 1988.

281. Comment by Warren Buffett, Berkshire Hathaway annual meeting, 1992 (As reported in "How to Buffett Against the Perils of Perots," Herb Ross, *Westfield Leader*, August 6, 1992.)

282. Robert Lenzner, "Warren Buffett's Idea of Heaven: I don't have to work with people I don't like," *Forbes 400*, October 18, 1993, p. 40.

283. L. J. Davis, "Buffett Takes Stock," *The New York Times Magazine*, April 1, 1990, p. 16.

284. Warren Buffett, "You Pay a Very High Price in the Stock Market for a Cheery Consensus," *Forbes*, August 6, 1979, p. 25.

285. Robert Lenzner, "Warren Buffett's Idea of Heaven: I don't have to work with people I don't like," *Forbes 400*, October 18, 1993, p. 40.

286. L .J. Davis, "Buffett Takes Stock," *The New York Times Magazine*, April 1, 1990, p. 16.

287. Linda Grant, "The $4-Billion Regular Guy," *The Los Angeles Times Magazine*, April 7, 1991, p. 34.

288. *Forbes 400*, September 13, 1982, p. 116.

289. Warren Buffett letter to partners, January 20, 1966.

290. Jim Rasmussen, "Hometown Deal Pleases Buffett," *Omaha World-Herald*, October 21, 1992, p. 16.

291. Berkshire Hathaway annual meeting, Omaha, May 6, 1996

292. Adam Smith, "The Modest Billionaire," *Esquire*, October 1988, p. 103.

293. Warren Buffett, *Nightly Business Report*, PBS, December 13, 1994.

294. David Elsner, "It Works: Buying $1 for 40 cents," *Chicago Tribune*, December 8, 1985, Section 7, p. 1.

295. Alan Gersten, "Buffett Faces Shareholders," *Omaha World-Herald*, May 21, 1986, p. 27.

296. Ann Hughey, "Omaha's Plain Dealer," *Newsweek*, April 1, 1985, p. 56.

297. Andrew Kilpatrick, *Of Permanent Value: The Story of Warren Buffett*, (Birmingham, AKPE, 1994), p. 568.

298. Warren Buffett, "What We Can Learn from Phil Fisher," *Forbes*, October 19, 1987, p. 40.

299. Terence P. Pare, "Yes, You Can Beat the Market," *Fortune*, April 3, 1995.

300. Warren Buffett letter, April 15, 1994. Shared by Walter Schloss.

301. Warren Buffett and Walter Schloss, discussion, New York Society of Security Analysts, December 6, 1994.

302. Andrew Kilpatrick, *Of Permanent Value: The Story of Warren Buffett*, (Birmingham: AKPE, 1994) p. 62.

303. Berkshire Hathaway annual meeting, Omaha, May 1, 1995.

304. Maria Mallory, "Behemoth on a Tear," *Business Week*, October 3, 1994.

305. Warren E. Buffett, "How Inflation Swindles the Equity Investor," *Fortune*, May 5, 1977, p. 250.

306. Robert Lenzner, "The Secrets of Salomon," *Forbes*, November 23, 1992, p. 123.

307. Warren Buffett, "You Pay a Very High Price in the Stock Market for a Cheery Consensus," *Forbes*, August 6, 1979, p. 15.

308. Warren E. Buffett, "The Security I Like Best," *The Commercial and Financial Chronicle*, December 6, 1951.

309. Jim Rasmussen, "Buffett Talks Strategy with Students," *Omaha World-Herald*, January 2, 1994, p. 17S.

310. Ibid.

311. Warren Buffett, Letter to Rep. John Dingell, D-MI, chairman of the House subcommittee on oversight and investigations, March, 1982.

312. Ibid.

313. "Look at All Those Beautiful, Scantily Clad Girls Out There!" *Forbes*, November 1, 1974.

314. Brett Duval Fromson, "Are These the New Warren Buffetts?" *Fortune*, *1990 Investor's Guide*, p. 81.

315. Adam Smith, "The Modest Billionaire," *Esquire*, October, 1988, p. 103.

316. Warren Buffett, letter to John Dingell, chairman of the House of Representatives Subcommittee on Oversight and Investigations, March 1982.

317. Brett Duval Fromson, "Warm Tip from Warren Buffett: It's Time to Buy Freddie Macs," *Fortune*, December 19, 1988, p. 33.

318. Berkshire Hathaway annual meeting, Omaha, 1993.

319. Linda Grant, "Striking Out at Wall Street," *U.S. News & World Report*, June 20, 1994, p. 58.

320. Robert Lenzner and David S. Fondiller, "Meet Charlie Munger," *Forbes*, January 22, 1996.

321. Warren E. Buffett, "How to Solve Our Trade Mess without Ruining Our Economy," *The Washington Post*, May 3, 1987, p. B1.

322. Berkshire Hathaway annual meeting, Omaha, 1996.

323. John C. Coffee, Jr. Louis Lowenstein, and Susan Ackerman, eds., *Knights, Raiders, and Targets*, (New York: Oxford University Press, 1988) pp. 11–27.

324. Tatiana Pouschine with Carolyn Torcellini, "Will the Real Warren Buffett Please Stand Up," *Forbes*, March 19, 1990, p. 92.

325. "Warren Buffett Talks Business," The University of North Carolina, Center for Public Television, Chapel Hill, 1995.

326. "Warren Buffett's $2-Billion Song and Dance," *Fortune*, March 4, 1996.

327. Gary Strauss, "Buffett's a Buddy to Targeted firms," *USA Today*, August 9, 1989.

328. Linda Grant, "Striking Out at Wall Street," *U.S. News & World Report*, June 20, 1994, p. 58.

329. Linda Grant, "The $4-Billion Regular Guy," *The Los Angeles Times Magazine*, April 7, 1991.

330. Frequently quoted. The author heard the comment at the 1994 Berkshire Hathaway annual meeting in Omaha.

331. Warren E. Buffett, "How Inflation Swindles the Equity Investor," *Fortune*, May 5, 1977, p. 250.

332. Robert Dorr, "Investor Warren Buffett Views Making Money as 'Big Game,'" *Omaha World-Herald*, March 21, 1985, p. 1.

333. Robert Dorr, "Buffett Acknowledges Risk Factor in His Purchase of WPPSS Bonds," *Omaha World-Herald*, April 15, 1985.

334. Warren Buffett, "Investing in Equity Markets," quoted in Columbia University Business School, transcript of a seminar held March 13, 1985, p. 19.

335. Linda Grant, "Striking Out at Wall Street," *U.S. News & World Report*, June 20, 1994, p. 58.

336. Adam Smith, "The Modest Billionaire," *Esquire*, October 1988, p. 103.

337. Linda Grant, "Striking Out at Wall Street," *U.S. News & World Report*, June 20, 1994, p. 58.

338. Ann Hughey, "Omaha's Plain Dealer," *Newsweek*, April 1, 1985, p. 56.

339. James Fogarty, "Buffett Questioned in IBM Suit," *Omaha World-Herald*, January 24, 1980, p. C1.

340. Warren Buffett, "Investing in Equity Markets," quoted in Columbia University Business School, transcript of a seminar held March 13, 1985, p. 23.

341. Linda Grant, "The $4-Billion Regular Guy," *The Los Angeles Times Magazine*, April 7, 1991, p. 36.

342. Linda Grant, "Striking Out at Wall Street," *U.S. News & World Report*, June 20, 1994, p. 58.

343. David A. Vise and Steve Coll, "Buffett-watchers Follow Lead of Omaha's Long-term Stock Investor," *The Washington Post*, October 2, 1987, p. D1.

344. Warren Buffett, "Reforming Casino Society," *Financial World*, January 20, 1987, p. 138, reprinted from *The Washington Post*.

345. Michael Lewis, "The Temptation of St. Warren," *The New Republic*, February 17, 1992, p. 22.

346. Robert Lenzner and Davis S. Fondiller, "The Not-So-Silent Partner," *Forbes*, January 22, 1996, p. 78.

347. "Warren Edward Buffett," *Forbes 400*, October 21, 1991, p. 151.

348. Berkshire Hathaway annual meeting, Omaha, May 1, 1995.

349. Robert Dorr, "Buffett Quickly Unloaded First Three Stock Shares," *Omaha World-Herald*, December 5, 1968.

350. "Warren Buffett Talks Business," The University of North Carolina, Center for Public Television, Chapel Hill, 1995.

351. Berkshire Hathaway annual meeting, Omaha, 1988.

352. "Warren Buffett Talks Business," The University of North Carolina, Center for Public Television, Chapel Hill, 1995.

353. "Look at All Those Beautiful, Scantily Clad Girls Out There!" *Forbes*, November 1, 1974.

354. Jim Rasmussen, "Billionaire Talks Strategy with Students," *Omaha World-Herald*, January 2, 1994, p. 17S.

355. Berkshire Hathaway annual meeting, Omaha, May 1, 1995.

356. Warren Buffett, "Investing in Equity Markets," quoted in Columbia University Business School, transcript of a seminar held March 13, 1985, pp. 28–29.

357. Robert Lenzner, "Warren Buffett's Idea of Heaven: I don't work with people I don't like," *Forbes 400*, October 18, 1993, p. 40.

358. "Warren Buffett Talks Business," The University of North Carolina, Center for Public Television, Chapel Hill, 1995.

359. Associated Press and The New York Times News Services, "Buffett Buys Out the Rest of GEICO," *The San Diego Union-Tribune*, August 26, 1995, p. C1.

360. "The Appeal of a Lousy Business," *Forbes*, March 19, 1990, p. 96.

361. Robert Dorr, "Buffett Says Firm's Performance Is 'Certain to Decline.'" *Omaha World-Herald*, May 22, 1984, p. C1.

362. Berkshire Hathaway annual meeting, Omaha, 1993.

363. Jim Rasmussen, "Billionaire Talks Strategy with Students," *Omaha World-Herald*, January 2, 1994, p. 17S.

364. "Warren Buffett Talks Business," The University of North Carolina, Center for Public Television, Chapel Hill, 1995.

365. Bob Reilly, "The Richest Man in America," *USWest*, Autumn, 1987, p. 2.

366. "How Omaha Beats Wall Street," *Forbes*, November 1, 1969, p. 82.

367. "Warren Buffett Talks Business," The University of North Carolina, Center for Public Television, Chapel Hill, 1995.

368. Roger Lowenstein, *Buffett: The Making of an American Capitalist*, (New York: Random House, 1995) p. 234.

369. Warren Buffett speech, New York Society of Security Analysts, December 6, 1996.

370. Berkshire Hathaway annual meeting, Omaha, April 29, 1991.

371. Robert Dorr, "Buffett's Ad Seeks Businesses to Purchase," *Omaha World-Herald*, November 18, 1986, p. C1.

372. "Warren Buffett Triples Profits," *New York Post*, May 14, 1994, p. D1.

373. Brett Duval Fromson, "Are These the New Warren Buffetts?" *Fortune, 1990 Investor's Guide*, p. 82.

374. Comments by Warren Buffett, Berkshire Hathaway annual meeting, Omaha, 1992.

375. Mark Hulbert, "Be a Tiger, Not a Hen," *Forbes*, May 25, 1992, p. 298.

376. Berkshire Hathaway annual meeting, Omaha, 1996.

377. Berkshire Hathaway annual meeting, Omaha, May 21, 1984.

378. "Warren Buffett Talks Business," The University of North Carolina, Center for Public Television, Chapel Hill, 1995.

379. *The Wall Street Journal*, September 30, 1987, p. 17.

380. Robert Dorr, "Buffett's Ad Seeks Businesses to Purchase," *Omaha World-Herald*, November 18, 1986.

381. Terence P. Pare, "Yes, You Can Beat the Market," *Fortune*, April 3, 1995.

382. Roger Lowenstein, *Buffett: The Making of an American Capitalist*, (New York: Random House, 1995) p. 132.

383. Advertisement, *The Wall Street Journal*, Monday, November 17, 1986, p. 16.

384. Berkshire Hathaway annual meeting, Omaha, 1989.

385. Warren Buffett speech, New York Society of Security Analysts, December 6, 1994.

386. Berkshire Hathaway annual meeting, Omaha, 1993.

387. Warren Buffett speech, New York Society of Security Analysts, December 6, 1994.

388. L. J. Davis, "Buffett Takes Stock," *The New York Times Magazine*, April 1, 1990, p. 16.

389. Warren Buffett speech, New York Society of Security Analysts, December 6, 1994.

390. Carol J. Loomis, "The Inside Story of Warren Buffett," *Fortune*, April 11, 1988, p. 26.

391. Berkshire Hathaway annual meeting, Omaha, 1991.

392. Berkshire Hathaway annual meeting, Omaha, May 6, 1996.

393. Alan C. Greenberg, *Memos from the Chairman*, (New York: Workman Publishing, 1996).

394. Patricia E. Bauer, "The Convictions of a Long-Distance Investor," *Channels*, November, 1986, p. 22.

395. Ibid.

396. "Lights! Camera! Cash Flow!" *Fortune*, September 6, 1993, p. 11.

397. Alan Bersten, "Buffett Faces Shareholders," *Omaha World-Herald*, May 21, 1986, p. 27.

398. Berkshire Hathaway annual meeting, Omaha, 1994.

399. Berkshire Hathaway annual meeting, Omaha, 1996.

400. Judith H. Dobrzynski, "Warren's World," *Business Week*, May 10, 1993, p. 30.

401. Robert Dorr, "Buffett Says Firm's Performance 'Is Certain to Decline,'" *Omaha World-Herald*, May 22, 1985, p. C1.

402. Gary Weiss and David Greising, "Poof! Wall Street's Sorcerers Lose Their Magic," *Business Week*, January 27, 1992, p. 74.

403. Claude Bejet, "Coke and Candy," *Forbes*, June 19, 1995, p. 152.

404. "The New Establishment 50," *Vanity Fair*, October, 1995, p. 280.

405. Robert Lenzner, "Warren Buffett's Idea of Heaven: I don't have to work with people I don't like," *Forbes 400*, October 18, 1993, p. 40.

406. Berkshire Hathaway annual meeting, Omaha, May 6, 1996.

407. Ibid.

408. Ibid.

409. Warren Buffett speech, New York Society of Security Analysts, December 6, 1994.

410. L. J. Davis, "Buffett Takes Stock," *The New York Times Magazine*, April 1, 1990, p. 16.

411. "Buffett Wins Berkshire Approval for Cheaper Stock, Urges Patience," *The Los Angeles Times*, May 7, 1996, p. D3.

412. Ibid.

413. Ann Kates, "Berkshire Hathaway Joins NYSE," *USA Today*, November 8, 1988.

414. Frank Lalli, "Buffett's New Stock: Looks great . . . but is less filling," *Money*, April 1996, p. 94.

415. Reed Abelson, "Market Place," *The New York Times*, May 8, 1996, p. D4.

416. Frank Lalli, "Buffett's New Stock: Looks great . . . but is less filling," *Money*, April, 1996, p. 94.

417. Walter Hamilton, "Investor's Corner," *Investors Business Daily*, February 23, 1996.

418. Ibid.

419. Alan Abelson, "Manchurian Capitalist," *Barron's*, April 22, 1996, p.1.

420. Malcolm Berko, "If Buffett Won't Buy Shares, Why Should You?" *San Diego Business Journal*, July 15, 1996, p. 41.

421. Irving Kahn commentary, New York Society of Security Analysts, December 6, 1996.

422. Warren Buffett, "Oil Discovered in Hell," *Investment Decisions*, May 1985, p. 22.

423. Alan Gersten, "Buffett Tells Shareholders What He Seeks in Firms," *Omaha World-Herald*, May 21, 1986, p. D1.

424. Berkshire Hathaway annual meeting, Omaha, 1987.

425. "Warren Buffett Talks Business," The University of North Carolina, Center for Public Television, Chapel Hill, 1995.

426. Carol J. Loomis, "Buffett to Disney: All Thumbs Up," *Fortune*, April 4, 1996, p. 35.

427. Warren Buffett speech, New York Society of Security Analysts, December 6, 1994.

428. Ibid.

429. "Warren Buffett Talks Business," The University of North Carolina, Center for Public Television, Chapel Hill, 1995.

430. Ibid.

431. Robert Dorr, *Omaha World-Herald*, October 20, 1991, p. D1.

432. Berkshire Hathaway annual meeting, Omaha, April 27, 1992.

433. Berkshire Hathaway annual meeting, Omaha, 1994.

434. "Warren Edward Buffett," *Forbes 400*, October 21, 1991, p. 151.

435. *Institutional Investor*, September 1991, as quoted by Andrew Kilpatrick, in *Of Permanent Value: The Story of Warren Buffett,* (Birmingham: APKE, 1994) p. 307.

436. Andrew Kilpatrick, *Of Permanent Value: The Story of Warren Buffett,* (Birmingham: AKPE, 1994) p. 310.

437. Linda Grant, "How Buffett Cleaned Up Salomon," *U.S. News & World Report*, June 20, 1994, p. 64.

438. Berkshire Hathaway annual meeting, Omaha, 1991.

439. Berkshire Hathaway annual meeting, Omaha, May 1, 1995.

440. "Warren Buffett Talks Business," The University of North Carolina, Center for Public Television, Chapel Hill, 1995.

441. "How Omaha Beats Wall Street," *Forbes*, November 1, 1969, p. 88.

442. Berkshire Hathaway annual meeting, Omaha, 1996.

443. Bill Gates, "What I Learned from Warren Buffett," *Harvard Business Review*, January/February, 1996, p. 148. Copyright 1995, Microsoft Corp.

444. Warren Buffett comments, Berkshire Hathaway annual meeting, Omaha, 1992.

445. Melissa Turner, *The Atlanta Constitution* as quoted by Andrew Kilpatrick, in *Of Permanent Value: The Story of Warren Buffett,* (Birmingham: APKE, 1994) p. 198.

446. Robert Lenzner, "Warren Buffett's Idea of Heaven: I don't have to work with people I don't like," *Forbes 400*, October 18, 1993, pg. 40.

447. Bernice Kanner, "Aw Shucks, It's Warren Buffett," *New York Magazine*, April 22, 1985, p. 52.

448. Berkshire Hathaway annual meeting, Omaha, 1996.

449. Sam Thornton, "Warren Buffett, Omahan in Search of Social Challenges," Lincoln, Nebraska, *Journal and Star*, March 18, 1973, p. 6F.

450. Berkshire Hathaway annual meeting, Omaha, May 1, 1995.

451. Berkshire Hathaway annual meeting, Omaha, May 1, 1995.

452. L. J. Davis, "Buffett Takes Stock," *The New York Times Magazine*, April 1, 1990.

453. Robert Dorr, "Buffett Says Firm's Performance Is 'Certain to Decline,'" *Omaha World-Herald*, May 22, 1984.

454. "Warren Buffett Talks Business," The University of North Carolina, Center for Public Television, Chapel Hill, 1995.

455. Ibid.

456. Ibid.

457. Ibid.

458. John Huey, "The World"s Best Brand," *Fortune*, May 31, 1993, p. 44.

459. Ibid.

460. "Now Hear This," *Fortune*, April 10, 1989, p. 21

461. Warren Buffett, "Investing in Equity Markets," quoted in Columbia University Business School, transcript of a seminar held March 13, 1985, pp. 11–12.

462. Bryan Burrough and John Helyar, *Barbarians at the Gate*, (Harper & Row: New York, 1990).

463. Jim Rasmussen, "Billionaire Talks Strategy with Students," *Omaha World-Herald*, January 2, 1994, p. 17S.

464. Patricia E. Bauer, "The Convictions of a Long-distance Investor," *Channel*s, November, 1986, p. 22.

465. Berkshire Hathaway annual meeting, Omaha, 1996.

466. Ibid.

467. Brett Duval Fromson, "Warm Tip from Warren Buffett: It's Time to Buy Freddie Macs," *Fortune*, December 19, 1988, p. 33.

468. *Courier-Express v. Evening News*, testimony of Warren Buffett, pp. 50–52.

469. Jim Rasmussen, "Billionaire Talks Strategy with Students," *Omaha World-Herald*, January 2, 1994, p. 17S.

470. *Fortune*, April 11, 1991.

471. Berkshire Hathaway annual meeting, Omaha, 1992.

472. Robert Lenzner, "Warren Buffett's Idea of Heaven: I don't have to work with people I don't like," *Forbes 400*, October 18, 1993, p. 40.

473. Jim Rasmussen, "Billionaire Talks Strategy with Students," *Omaha World-Herald*, January 2, 1994, p. 17S.

474. Linda Grant, "The $4-Billion Regular Guy," *The Los Angeles Times Magazine*, April 17, 1991, p. 36.

475. Robert Lenzner, "Warren Buffett's Idea of Heaven: I don't have to work with people I don't like," *Forbes 400*, October 18, 1993, p. 40.

476. A paraphrase of Warren Buffett's statement at the Berkshire Hathaway Annual Meeting, April 29, 1991.

477. Berkshire Hathaway annual meeting, Omaha, 1996.

478. Warren Buffett speech, New York Society of Security Analysts, December 6, 1996.

479. Linda Grant, "The $4-Billion Regular Guy," *The Los Angeles Times Magazine*, April 7, 1991, p. 36.

480. David A. Vise and Steve Coll, "Buffett-Watchers Follow Lead of Omaha's Long-term Stock Investor," *The Washington Post*, October 2, 1987, p. D1.

481. Berkshire Hathaway annual meeting, Omaha,1996.

482. Alan Gersten, "Buffett Faces Shareholders," *Omaha World-Herald*, May 21, 1986, p. 27.

483. Robert Dorr, "Newspaper Holdings Kind to Omaha Investor Buffett," *Omaha World-Herald*, April 16, 1978, p. 6J.

484. "Warren Buffett Talks Business," The University of North Carolina, Center for Public Television, Chapel Hill, 1995.

485. Jim Rasmussen, "Billionaire Talks Strategy with Students," *Omaha World-Herald,* January 2, 1994.

486. Linda Grant, "Striking Out at Wall Street," *U.S. News & World Report,* June 20, 1994, p. 58.

487. Andrew Kilpatrick, *Of Permanent Value: The Story of Warren Buffett,* (Birmingham: AKPE, 1994) p. 568, quoting from *Forbes,* August 6, 1990.

488. Robert McMorris, "Investor Buffett Tells Secret: Follow Will Rogers' Advice," *Omaha World-Herald,* May 31, 1985, p. B1.

489. Warren E. Buffett, "How Inflation Swindles the Equity Investor," *Fortune,* May 5, 1977, p. 250.

490. Warren Buffett, 1988 Capital Cities/ABC management conference.

491. Berkshire Hathaway annual meeting, Omaha, 1996

492. "Warren Buffett Talks Business," The University of North Carolina, Center for Public Television, Chapel Hill, 1995. (Modified later by Buffett letter to author.)

493. "Warren Buffett—The Pragmatist." *Esquire,* June, 1988, p. 159.

494. Warren E. Buffett, "Kiewit Legacy as Unusual as His Life," *Omaha World-Herald,* January 20, 1980, p. 1.

495. Walter Isaacson, "In Search of the Real Bill Gates," *Time,* January, 13, 1997, p. 57.

496. Sharon Rosse, "Buffett Foundation to Reward Teachers," *Omaha World-Herald,* October 1, 1987, p. 1.

497. Ibid.

498. Susan Buffett interview with the author, October, 1996.

499. Berkshire Hathaway annual report, Omaha,1994.

500. Warren Buffett, "Reforming Casino Society," *Financial World,* January 20, 1987, p. 139, (reprinted from *The Washington Post).*

501. Berkshire Hathaway annual meeting, Omaha, 1996.

502. Warren Buffett, letter to the author, October 23, 1989.

PERMISSIONS

Permission has been granted by the following organizations for quotes appearing in this book:

Adam Smith, for quotes taken from *Supermoney*.

The Associated Press

Warren Buffett

Channels

Excerpts from *Forbes Magazine*, reprinted by permission of *Forbes Magazine* © FORBES, Inc.

Fortune Magazine, © 1977, 1988, 1990, 1992 Time, Inc. All rights reserved.

Investment Decisions

Of Permanent Value: The Story of Warren Buffett, © 1994 by Andrew Kilpatrick, reprinted by permission of the author.

Buffett: The Making of an American Capitalist by Roger Lowenstein, reprinted by permission of Random House, © 1995.

Los Angeles Times

Microsoft Corporation

New York Magazine

New York Times Magazine

Omaha World-Herald

Outstanding Investor Digest

PBS Nightly Business Report

Regardie's

U.S. News and World Report, © June 20, 1994.

U.S. West Magazine

"Legend Revisited: Warren Buffett's Aura ..." reprinted by permission of *The Wall Street Journal,* © 1996 Dow Jones & Company, Inc. All rights reserved worldwide.

Warren Buffett Talks Business, text reprinted with permission by the PBS television program, produced by the North Carolina Center for Public Television, 1995.

The Washington Post

Worth